E-Learning Games

Interactive Learning Strategies
for Digital Delivery

Kathleen M. Iverson, Ph.D.
Roosevelt University

**International Academy of
Design & Technology**
39 John Street
Toronto, Ontario M5V 3G6

PEARSON

Prentice
Hall

Upper Saddle River, New Jersey

Library of Congress Cataloging-in-Publication Data

Iverson, Kathleen M.
    E-Learning games : interactive learning strategies for digital delivery / Kathleen M. Iverson
        p. cm.
    Includes bibliographical references and index.
    ISBN 0-13-097943-0
    1. Web-based instruction. 2. Educational games. 3. Active learning. I. Title.

LB1044.87.I94 2005
371.33'7–dc22

2004044343

Director of Production and Manufacturing: Bruce Johnson
Executive Editor: Elizabeth Sugg
Editorial Assistant: Cyrenne Bolt de Freitas
Marketing Manager: Leigh Ann Sims
Managing Editor–Production: Mary Carnis
Manufacturing Buyer: Ilene Sanford
Production Liason: Denise Brown
Full-Service Production/Composition: Carlisle Publishers Services
Design Director: Cheryl Asherman
Senior Design Coordinator/Cover Design: Christopher Weigand
Cover Printer: Phoenix Color
Printer/Binder: RR Donnelley & Sons

Pearson Education Ltd.
Pearson Education Singapore, Pte. Ltd.
Pearson Education Canada, Ltd.
Pearson Education—Japan
Pearson Education Australia PTY, Limited
Pearson Education North Asia Ltd.
Pearson Educación de México, S.A. de C.V.
Pearson Education Malaysia, Pte. Ltd.

10 9 8 7 6 5 4 3 2 1
ISBN 0-13-097943-0

Contents

Preface

The mere imparting of information is not education. Above all things, the effort must result in making a man think and do for himself.

—Carter G. Woodson

A guiding principle that most educators and trainers agree upon is that education is not information, and this premise holds true in both traditional and electronic delivery. As classroom trainers and teachers, we know that we must actively engage our participants if we are to keep them motivated and involved in the learning process. How do we take the same active, accelerated, collaborative techniques that have made our classroom training come alive and apply them to a web-based environment? *E-Learning Games* fills a significant gap in the web-based training design literature by offering a variety of active learning games, simulations, openers, closers, content review exercises, and idea generators that can be readily implemented in most online courses. These activities will engage learners from their very first click and keep them coming back for more. If you believe that learning happens through interaction and collaboration and is a dynamic, creative process that involves the true exchange of ideas, not simply the accumulation of facts with precious little guidance on how to apply them, then you will find the principles in this book useful. The practices presented in *E-Learning Games* facilitate interaction and collaboration so that designers might create dynamic e-learning courses that put learners in the driver's seat of their development.

E-learning naysayers have expressed valid concerns about the cost, engagement, and quality of e-learning, frequently stating, "It is too expensive. I can't spend $50,000 designing a ten-minute training program!" "It's boring. My learners will fall asleep at their computer screens." "My students won't learn as much as they will in the classroom." As designers and educators, we must overcome this negativity with quality, low cost, and highly effective courseware. The goal of this book is to guide the rapid design and delivery of interesting, engaging, highly interactive e-learning environments that facilitate knowledge construction.

Until recently, most interaction in web-based training environments was technologically driven. Intelligent tutors, video, audio, and animated graphics were the accepted vehicles for adding interest and excitement to otherwise bland and boring script-based training. Although these advances are valuable, they come with a price in both development time and dollars. *E-Learning Games* contains ideas and practices that will add excitement to courseware without considerable expenditure of resources. Relying primarily on low-tech vehicles such as synchronous and asynchronous chat, e-mail, and instant messaging, the activities described in this textbook can be implemented in web-based training and educational courses alike.

In using this book, begin by carefully reviewing Chapters 1 through 3 to gain perspective on the premises that guide interactivity and motivation in e-learning. Here you will review principles of constructivism, instruction design, and web-based interaction so that you might apply them to your courseware. You will find useful tables and checklists to help you quickly plan quality e-learning products. Chapters 4 through 10 contain games, exercises, activities, and simulations that may be readily added to your course content to generate opportunities for collaboration, practice, and knowledge creation.

The ideas presented here will put the "learning" back in your e-learning courseware, motivating your participants to put forth the effort to "think and do" as they construct valuable and useful knowledge.

Acknowledgments

Thanks to Roger Addison and Roger Chevalier, International Society for Performance Improvement; and Richard Osgood, Intellishare, LLC, for reviewing this text.

Author Bio
Kathleen Iverson, Ph.D.

Kathleen Iverson is Associate Professor of Training and Development at Roosevelt University located in Chicago, Illinois, where she designs and delivers both online and traditional courses to graduate students in e-learning and training design, delivery, and evaluation. Dr. Iverson helped initiate Roosevelt University's highly successful, fully online master's degree program to prepare students for careers in training, e-learning, and organization development. She holds a Ph.D. from Loyola University, Chicago, in Training and Organization Development. In addition to her academic work, she has published both theoretical and empirical studies relating to distance learning and has consulted to major corporations including Hotel Sofitel, Marriott, Alliant, Chicago Convention and Tourism Bureau, and McDonald's Corporation.

CHAPTER 1
Welcome to Active E-Learning

E-Learning Games is a resource tool that will help you design e-learning courses that are engaging and interactive. Here you will find games, simulation exercises, experiential activities, and other approaches that will add excitement to your e-learning courses without considerable expenditure of resources in the form of design time or technology. The strategies described herein will engage learners in a way that makes them want to learn. Because the strategies are constructivist in nature, much of the responsibility for interaction and knowledge development rests on the learners. Most strategies require you and the students to have only basic technology skills, as there is no streaming media, flash components, or java script writing invloved. Grounded in educational theory and highly interactive, the ideas in this textbook will enable you to create quality e-learning with a focus on design rather than bells and whistles. The simplicity of delivery reduces the learning curve for everyone involved, making e-learning a viable option when time and cost are at issue. You will, however, need a solid understanding of learning theory and instruction design principles, including assessment and analysis.

    E-Learning Games is based on a combination of research and practice. A broad body of literature regarding e-learning has been created in a short time. Variable opinions and ideas already exist about use of technology, program design, and delivery. As a culmination of reviewing hundreds of books and articles on learning at a distance, and designing and teaching an array of online courses, the following list provides important facts about e-learning.

Successful e-learning must be:

1. *Enjoyable and engaging.* Dropout rates are higher in distance learning environments, so we must create interesting courses that motivate learners to stick with it.
2. *Positive and supportive.* People learn best in a positive learning environment that is both relaxed and stimulating.
3. *Active.* People learn best when actively involved in practices that allow them to construct their own knowledge and understanding.
4. *Collaborative.* We must create a community of learners where peers support each other in their educational endeavors.

5. *Contextual.* We must immerse our learners in activities that are closely linked or identical to those that they perform in the real world.

The games and learning exercises in this textbook will help you realize these five principles in your e-learning courses. They will help you design courses that offer more than just information. This textbook will help you involve learners from the start, create realistic learning environments, facilitate knowledge development and retention, generate group interaction and peer support, and lead students to a workplace transfer.

How to Use this Book

The primary purpose of *E-Learning Games* is to bring together a collection of instructional strategies that may be included in an e-learning course design to prompt interactivity. It includes design ideas to get learners involved from the first click and keep them coming back. It also includes practices for stimulating discussion, full class and small group learning, subject matter review, and peer learning. *E-Learning Games* is for anyone who designs or teaches on the web. Although the book is directed toward trainers in professional fields, the activities may also be adapted to educational settings that involve older children or adults. The series of strategies within will enable you to bring your course content alive. E-learning that is only information based lacks excitement, motivating factors, interactivity, and fun.

This book assumes that you have conducted a thorough needs assessment and have identified the content that you will teach and the particular needs and characteristics of your learners. Consider each exercise to be an expanded frame that supplies an idea, directions for use, instructions for learners, and possible variations. The frames are not content related and may be adapted to an array of course topics and settings, but the decision on how and when to use them is up to you, the course developer.

Following this brief introduction, Chapter 2 will explore interactivity, the premise that guides this book. Here you will examine four types of interaction that occur in web-based learning and review strategies that will help you achieve success at each level. Next you will review constructivist design principles in Chapter 3 and examine specific strategies that you may use in planning interactive, constructivist learning on the web.

The techniques described throughout the remainder of this textbook are strategies that enable you to add interactivity to your subject matter. Chapter 4 contains icebreakers and opening activities that may be used during any online learning experience to encourage learners to take an immediate active role. The activities are designed to help those who are new to e-learning to become comfortable in an online environment before addressing content. Experienced e-learners enjoy having an opportunity to meet classmates virtually and begin communicating. Chapter 5 introduces learning scenarios that may be added to courses without the necessity of expensive technology and design. These include how to introduce and guide simulated learning, problem-based learning approaches, role play, and case study. Chapter 6 provides exercises to instigate and facilitate peer learning, a powerful component of e-learning. Chapter 7 examines a variety of active learning exercises that encourage learners to explore and practice the course content. Chapter 8 contains prompts for virtual discussion and Chapter 9 has strategies for idea generation and creativity. Finally, because the way a course ends is just as important as the way it begins, Chapter 10 contains closers that reinforce transfer and prompt continued learning.

Each activity contains clearly written instructions that you may add directly to your course, with suggestions for possible variation. The accompanying recommendations for free software trials or shareware enable or enhance some exercises. (The author does not represent any of the providers but simply offers them to you as suggestions.) The exercises do not recommend a specific audience, because this important decision is best left to you, the designer or facilitator, who has assessment information regarding the individual characteristics of your learners. Each activity suggests ways that you might evaluate your learners, but these are only suggestions. The important task of evaluation should directly address your particular course's learning objectives and content. Note also that some of the activities are game based, and thus can lead to competition between learners. You may increase or decrease the competitive spirit of the games by varying the performance rewards or outcomes. You may choose to recognize more than just correct answers (participation, time on task, most creative answer, and so forth). For example, you may require all students to participate to some degree in forums, but do not assign a grade to each post or require all students to participate in all activities. In addition, although each activity contains an objective, feel free to use your particular measurable course and learning objectives based on your learners, course content, and organizational goals.

Following are additional suggestions for implementing the activities in Chapters 4 through 10.

- ◆ Consider your audience. Conduct a pretest of knowledge, skill, and ability before you enroll users to determine their skill in technology and knowledge of course content.
- ◆ Revise exercises to meet the needs of your audience.
- ◆ Develop measurable objectives for each exercise and relate them to your evaluation.
- ◆ Be available to facilitate online discussion, provide feedback, and answer questions.
- ◆ Provide prompt feedback regarding performance.
- ◆ Add additional web resources to link your content to the activities.
- ◆ Start slow. It is better to add activity to a course as it proceeds than to overwhelm learners at the start. (See Chapter 2, "Balancing Interaction," for more on this.)

The strategies in this book are simple, yet powerful, vehicles for knowledge construction. When infused into online courses, they can provide a wealth of positive response from learners and internal and external course evaluators. Students are amazed at how much they can learn and retain from an online course, how well they get to know other learners, and how active they can be in an asynchronous, web-based environment.

CHAPTER 2
Interactive E-Learning

Creating and managing interaction in online courses is the essence of rich educational experience. You cannot simulate the rapport experienced in traditional training: the uproarious laughter when a good joke is shared, a round of spontaneous applause for a trainee who achieves a breakthrough, or the pleasure of sharing bagels or doughnuts in an early morning session. Yet you can maximize the fun, adventure, and opportunity for connection that e-learning brings. The vehicle that allows you to breathe life into online learning is *interactivity*. Courses that lack this component are dry and leave learners searching for an escape route. For example, the practice of placing 100 text-based PowerPoint slides in a course followed by a few quizzes is not e-learning, it is e-boring.

What exactly is interaction in e-learning? According to Wagner, interaction is an interplay and exchange in which individuals and groups influence each other. Thus, interaction is when there are "reciprocal events requiring two objects and two actions."[1] Your role as instructional designer is to move from merely sequencing material to creating highly interactive online environments in which constructivist learning may occur by creating opportunities for groups and individuals to influence one another. Such environments present rich contexts, authentic tasks, collaboration for the development and evaluation of multiple perspectives, an abundance of tools to enhance communication and access to real-world examples and problems, reflective thinking, modeling or problem solving by experts in the content domain, and mentoring relationships to guide learning.[2] The planning, implementation, and management of learner interaction is paramount to the success of e-learning. Studies show that the perception of interaction is a critical predictor of course success and that interaction is valued by learners.[3] For example, consider the online delivery of a course on sexual harassment. Learners must read material, take brief quizzes, and move through the course content without the benefit of an instructor or other learner contact. As long as they score a 90% or better on the quiz, they are deemed literate in this topic. But do they truly understand the issue, views, and implications of sexual harassment after reading a few screens and taking a quiz? It is much more effective to place learners in groups where they receive guidance on how to use web resources to explore the topic, discuss their findings with others, work together to locate answers, create their own model of sexual harassment prevention, and receive feedback and further guidance from a facilitator.

5

A Closer Look at Interactivity

Each event that is connected to an instructional strategy or goal is an interaction, or a transaction, that occurs between the learner and other human or technological resources. Interaction allows trainees to experience the content, making them active participants in the learning process rather than passive bystanders. Interactivity in e-learning does the following:

- ◆ Differentiates an e-learning course from a self-study or correspondence course
- ◆ Allows participants to define and construct knowledge
- ◆ Creates a learning community
- ◆ Provides feedback
- ◆ Stimulates and motivates learners
- ◆ Promotes social experiences rather than independent ones

If you want to create and manage a highly interactive learning environment, then you must clearly understand what the term *interactivity* implies.

Classes of Interaction

Four classes of communication-based interaction in e-learning environments have been identified that may be delivered synchronously or asynchronously. These include interactions that involve the learner and the interface or delivery system,[4] the learner and content, the learner and facilitator, and the learner and other learners.[5] Table 2.1 contains interactive components that correspond to each of the four levels. Let us examine each class of interaction in detail.

Learner-Interface Interaction

Learner-interface interaction in online learning is the process of manipulating technological tools to accomplish a task.[6] This basic component differentiates e-learning from other forms of learning at a distance that do not involve the support of technology such as correspondence study, independent study, or other print-based, self-directed learning. To be successful, trainees must first master learner-interface components if they are to move ahead and experience interaction with content, peers, and instructors. The learner-interface interaction provides access to instruction and permits learners to participate in other essential learner interactions. If learner-interface interaction fails, then trainees will be unable to participate at any level in other learner interactions. In effect, adequate and reliable learner-interface interaction is the keystone to learner involvement; if it fails, training fails.

When considering learning-interface interaction, you must focus on both the skills and experience with technology that the learner brings to the course and also the interface or delivery platform you are using to teach the course.

Table 2.1
Interactivity in Course Design

Interaction	Component
Learner-interface	• Web-based resources: Hotlist, Virtual Field Trip, Webquest, etc. • E-storming
Learner-content	• Course objectives • Assignment descriptions • Opening scenario • Knowledge base • Textbook • Content review and practice exercises: Scavenger Hunt, Backward Quiz, Treasure Hunt, Twenty Questions, etc.
Learner-facilitator	• Invitation to learn • FAQ forum • Dear Abby forum • E-mail messages: Cheerleader, Ping, Thank you, Reminders • Feedback on assignments • Quick response to questions
Learner-learner	• Peer review and feedback • Group discussion: Jigsaw, Virtual Fishbowl, Process Facilitation, Projector and Screen • Peer learning: Buddy System, Secret Mentor, Storyboard, etc.

Learner Competency

Many novice facilitators of e-learning assume that trainees bring all the prerequisite knowledge of technology that they will need to grasp the interface, only to find that some learners lack basic skills that are necessary for successful learner-interface interaction. The only way to avoid this difficulty is to test computer competency as part of your learner assessment process. Following are three broad areas that must be assessed.

1. What level of computer and internet skill does your audience possess?
2. What types of e-learning experiences has your audience had in the past?
3. Does your audience have the technology available and ability to use all resources of the course you plan to deliver?

If answers to these questions indicate that your audience lacks prerequisite skills, then you must first address this deficiency with targeted training before moving on to more complex, job-specific course delivery. Once trainees have mastered these basic skills, they will have the prerequisite knowledge to move ahead and learn the particular interface used to deliver the course.

Quality of Interface

A second component of successful learner-interface interaction concerns the quality of the interface used to deliver your course. The ease with which learners master the delivery interface, or the program or system you are using to deliver your courseware, depends on intuitiveness. Poor learner-interface interaction distracts the learner from accessing content and communicating with others. Conversely, good learner-interface interaction allows the learner to focus on learning and communication rather than how to access instructional content and communicate with others.[7] A desirable outcome of the learner-interface interaction is to render the technology user friendly and transparent. Ideally, the access technology should quickly become an unobtrusive, transparent window through which the opportunity for meaningful training can pass; however, such an outcome requires planning and thoughtful consideration of both the skill level of the learners and the quality of the interface.

Learner-interface interaction can be promoted by quality graphic user interface (GUI) design. Principles of quality GUI are as follows:

- Familiar language
- Clear, concise instructions
- Consistent navigation, color, and formatting
- Adherence to principles of alignment and proximity
- Maintaining of learner orientation by use of tools such as site maps and accessible navigation buttons
- Use of necessary graphics and content only

Learner-Content Interaction

Learner-content interaction is the process of intellectually interacting with content to bring about changes in the learner's understanding, perspective, or cognitive structure.[8] This experience occurs within individual learners as they interact with the course content and material. Rich content that is highly engaging, thought provoking, and emotionally involving will result in greater cognitive activity. Although the delivery medium is important, it is not as vital as technology-driven developers have led you to believe. Instructional design has a greater impact on learner achievement than the medium used to deliver the content.[9] As you consider the development of media-based interactive content, you must also assess the return on investment for creating and maintaining costly multimedia courseware by asking if the resulting effect is worth the price. The exercises in the book are based on the principles of constructivist learning and will facilitate learner achievement without breaking your budget.

Engaging and Motivating Content

Your goal as an e-learning designer is to create rich, vivid learning activities that will imprint on both short- and long-term memory. Heightened motivation creates emotional content that increases retention and expands the time trainees will attend to the learning material. When engaged in highly motivating activities, learners experience immersion, reflection, flow, collaboration, learner control, curiosity, fantasy, and challenge.[10] Your willingness to create a spirit of adventure in your e-learning courses, as well as an attitude of togetherness, will help learners feel connected to the course material and to other learners. This textbook contains a multitude of games and scenario-based activities that will bring adventure and collaboration into your electronic learning environment. Following are additional low-risk, low-tech strategies that can add interest and excitement to your courses.

Embed learning activities in a theme. Start with a common theme or story that runs through the entire session or course to develop internal coherence. All activities should be related and serve as building blocks for the tasks to be addressed. Choose themes that interest your particular group of learners. Possible themes for e-learning courses include team sports, travel, and mysteries. For example, if you choose a sports theme, the term *coaches* could be your online support, *running the bases* might take learners through the content, and *runs, hits,* and *errors* might be a way of delivering feedback.[11] You might also add a *dugout* for online communication and discussion, *pregame meetings* for initial discussion of strategy, and *postgame celebrations* in the *locker room* to provide positive feedback.

Create overarching scenarios. Begin your course with a dramatic story or scenario that readily grabs learners' attention. Give participants a role to play in which they must overcome adversity or solve a complex problem either individually or in groups. Participants achieve course objectives as they resolve real-life problems or business challenges. A possible scenario for executive development might involve the decision to enter new markets, avoid a hostile takeover, or react to a severe external challenge such as September 11. Participants devise strategies in multiple areas of operation including staffing, investment, product development, and marketing. Technology can help you deliver the scenario and allow you to provide feedback based on choices and decisions. (See Chapter 5 for more about scenario learning and scenario writing.)

Do not overlook audio and music. Although streaming video may overwhelm the limited computer resources of many trainees, audio can pack a powerful punch without the delays and space requirements of video. Text alone communicates information, but music and audio can also communicate feeling. Adding music to e-learning courses can highlight dramatic moments. Imagine the shark's theme from *Jaws.* Music may also convey the mood (circus music for fun, Mozart for something more serious), be it anxious themes for test-taking, frightening music for a trip to the boss's office (or positive music depending on the characteristics of the boss), or uplifting music that celebrates a big win (imagine the theme from *Rocky* or *Chariots of Fire*).[12]

Use pictures and graphic organizers rather than text. Graphics are particularly important in e-learning because they are the only visual support available. Graphics can be enhanced by adding animation, through the creation of interactive pictures or maps, or the use of animation with explanatory text. (For more on graphics, see the Mindmaps exercise in Chapter 7.)

Use icebreakers.   Online learning should establish the norm of active participation early in the learning process. This textbook contains many useful icebreakers for any e-learning course. If time allows, include several icebreakers for both the entire class and small groups. Participate in the activities yourself so learners get to know you.

Speed up the pace of learning.   Online learning must have a rapid, varied pace that grabs and engages the learner. For example, there should be no more than two successive text-only screens before the learner is involved in an exercise. A text-only screen is tantamount to a lecture without the visual gestures and personality of the speaker. In other words, it is boring!

Combine interactive strategies.   Rather than relying on simple quizzes for interactivity, create a mix of games, puzzles, assessments, and scenarios throughout the course. You will find a wide array of interactive strategies in this textbook that facilitate discussion, problem solving, constructive thinking, and creativity.

Learner-Facilitator Interaction

Learner-facilitator interactions are purposed around the clarification of goals and content to motivate and stimulate the learner to succeed. They consist of trainee or instructor communication that occurs before, during, and after instruction. Following are the seven key learner-facilitator interactions that occur throughout the delivery of a course.[13]

1. Determine learning needs and preferences.
2. Establish learning outcomes and objectives.
3. Provide timely and appropriate feedback.
4. Facilitate information presentation.
5. Monitor and evaluate performance.
6. Facilitate learning activities.
7. Initiate, maintain, and facilitate discussion.

As this list indicates, you as a trainer in distance learning will be busy, perhaps spending twice as much time in delivering an e-learning course as you would in traditional training. Developing skill in both managing the quantity and quality of learner-facilitator interaction is important to course success. If you take a backseat right away, then trainees feel that they are in it alone, learning only from content or from each other. When you are highly involved, however, learners may never develop independence or self-direct their learning; and you can burn out quickly from the abundance of e-mail communications and discussion board posts that must be managed. Maintaining the correct level of involvement is important.

Following are strategies that will help you manage learner-facilitator interaction.

Specify your requirements.   Provide specific requirements for your course that relate to both knowledge development and participation. Be exact in specifying the frequency and duration of time that learners need to spend online. Let them know how often they must log in to the course site, check announcements, and post to the discussion board so there is no opportunity for misunderstanding.

Hold online office hours.   Identify specific times during the week when you will be online and available for questions from learners via e-mail or telephone. A specific schedule gives learners a sense of security and also allows you to more effectively manage your time.

Provide rich detail in your course design and instructions.   Learners must take in all instructions and information from print. You will not be present to answer questions and provide clarification, so deliver clear and detailed instructions up front to eliminate a multitude of e-mails from learners asking for clarification of objectives and requirements.

Create a "Frequently Asked Questions" section.   When questions from learners do arise, use them to develop an FAQ forum where learners can post questions and you provide answers. Instruct others in the class to check this forum first when they have questions. Also post questions and answers from previous classes here so learners can review them as needed.

Use the "Announcements" section.   Most online delivery platforms have an announcements section that is at the forefront of the course and can be quickly updated. Add new thoughts, ideas, links, or games to this section. Rather than sending broadcast e-mails, consider placing information in an announcement.

Limit discussion board presence.   Rather than responding to every post or adding lengthy thoughts and ideas to threads, get things started with an activity or game and then fade out. Add occasional brief, encouraging comments or clarifications to the discussion threads, but do not take over the boards.

Establish a pattern of frequent, quick response.   Check your e-mail often and answer questions or comments from learners within 24 hours. If you are going to be away for even a day or two, let everyone know ahead of time so they are prepared for possible response delays. Use short, private messages to keep communications alive, such as the following:

- *Return receipt messages,* which are sent to class members if you are busy, to tell them that you have received their message and will answer it soon
- *Cheerleader messages,* which recognize and praise exceptional efforts
- *Ping messages,* which ask participants who have not posted something recently to the group whether they are still participating

- *Thank-you messages,* which encourage participation when sent as interim expressions of appreciation
- *Reminder messages,* which serve to remind participants of approaching deadlines

Drive home value with feedback.   Learners deserve to know how they are doing, so provide detailed feedback on a timely basis. At the end of short activities, a general "good job" to the group or class as a whole can be delivered in the forum or in the announcements section. When individual or small group project work is completed, send personal feedback via e-mail to each participant.

Invent an e-coach.   Add a fictitious character who has "been there, done that" and delivers your course for you to the learners. Pedagogical agents are onscreen characters who guide the learner through the course. Your agent might be "Merv," who has completed this course successfully and is there to help guide the new learner and provide feedback. You might deliver your entire course as "Merv" or just have him jump in from time to time with suggestions and hints. Although we most typically think of agents as graphic characters, an agent's personality can be adequately communicated in text-based delivery.

Provide rewards and incentives.   Trainers often rely on tangible rewards to encourage class participation. Unfortunately, you cannot hand out candy bars to your e-learners when they provide the correct answers, but you can provide tangible e-awards to learners when they perform above and beyond expectations. There are many inexpensive rewards you can provide electronically via e-mail or send to learners via the postal service including candy, gift certificates, e-cards, and even a single share of stock. Make sure your reward is appropriate for your audience and is something that the learners would value.

Learner-Learner Interactions

Learner-learner interactions occur "between one learner and another learner, alone, or in group settings, with or without the real-time presence of an instructor."[14] Trainees may work together to analyze a problem, share information, voice opinions, and provide expertise. Peer interactions help groups and individuals construct and apply knowledge. The act of placing students in groups does not ensure effective collaboration. Clear identification of goals, group process, and careful monitoring of communication can facilitate effective peer interaction.

An Ethiopian proverb metaphorically illustrates the power that can be expressed among e-learners who collaborate in their learning: "When spider webs unite, they can tie up a lion." The following suggestions will help your class to start spinning its web.

Make it interesting.   The games and activities in this book all rely on learner-learner interaction. The immediacy they create will encourage learners to become highly involved in peer learning and course content.

Scaffold group work.   Begin with simple group assignments and move toward more complex, job-related group projects to allow learners time to become accustomed to e-group work.

Set norms for communication.   Review basic online communication principles such as netiquette to ensure that all understand the unique aspects of online interaction. Remind learners to never say anything online that they would not want to see on the front page of their local newspaper.

Provide electronic work group tools.   Encourage your e-groups to use electronic work group tools to facilitate discussions and team project work. See Addendum A for recommendations of shareware and free downloads of group tools and project management software.

Supply detailed expectations.   Be specific about the frequency and quality of interaction you expect learners to provide. Specify the frequency with which learners should interact with each other, that is, how often they should post, e-mail, or chat. Set a clear beginning and ending date for online discussion; all posts must be made by a certain date.

Make it easy to communicate.   Provide an e-mail distribution list for the course so everyone can reach each other. Encourage teams to use instant messaging and buddy lists.

Rotate responsibility for e-moderating.   Rather than you always acting as the e-moderator of online discussion, rotate this responsibility among learners. Provide clear guidelines and expectations and add support when needed.

Share project work.   Have groups deliver a tangible product (such as a report, public presentation, short videotape, or display) that is firmly scheduled, completed, and shared with all participants, and then made available to a larger, interested community. Provide opportunities for participants and their associates outside of the project group to marvel at what has been accomplished.

Plan for future collaboration.   Allow time and opportunity for thank-yous and good-byes and begin to speak about possibilities of working together in the future. (See the closing exercises in Chapter 10 for more ideas with regard to course endings.)

Table 2.2 contains a checklist that you may find helpful as you design your e-learning courses. It contains important criteria that are present in quality e-learning courseware.

Table 2.2
E-Learning Design Checklist

The following criteria are evident in quality e-learning courses.

Course Appearance
Page backgrounds are white or pale pastel with contrasting text colors and graphics.
Fonts are easy to read in both on-screen and printed versions.
Page size is at or near a standard 800 × 600 pixel resolution.
Screens take advantage of white space to display information on the page.
Graphics occupy minimum screen space and are used only to enhance the content.
Graphics file sizes are minimized for rapid loading.

Navigation
Site navigation is clearly specified so learners know where to find information.
Hyperlinks are attached to a few key words or a meaningful phrase.
Links and URLs are unambiguous, clear, and specific, and are as brief as possible.
Backward links are provided so that learners can return to their starting place.
Links to all software required for assignments and course completion are included.
Access to reference materials is provided or a knowledge base for independent research.
Content needed most often is in a prominent place.

Module Design
Course material is written in an active voice using first or second person and a conversational style.
All text is grammatically correct.
Assignments and projects are clearly described and include examples.
Learning objectives are clearly stated and describe the specific knowledge, skills, and abilities that learners will develop.
Each assignment, learning activity, or post is directly tied to a learning objective.
Each learning module includes an opportunity for the learner to practice and demonstrate acceptable performance and receive feedback.
Material is chunked in modules to facilitate retention.
Contains diverse interactivity opportunities that challenge learners.
Includes examples that are supported by analogies, metaphors, and stories.
Practice exercises include links that describe their theoretical or conceptual basis.
Material stimulates and facilitates collaboration with fellow learners.

Delivery
Course media requirements are consistent with software and hardware available to learners.
Allow ample time for course activities and assignments.
Progress and success are measured and tracked.
Engagement techniques are used to motivate learners.
Includes feedback from the instructor, peers, and self.

Instructor Support
Ready access to course instructor or mentor is necessary for quick response to questions.
Instructor holds online office hours.
Frequently Asked Questions forum is monitored by instructor.
Use announcement sections.
Provide frequent encouragement.
Rapid turnaround time on all assignments facilitates learning.
Initiate, maintain, and facilitate discussion.

Balancing Interaction

Designing an online course is akin to preparing a fine meal. Course content that is based on goals and learner objectives provides the basic ingredients for the meal; but without the addition of spice and flavoring, the meal will be bland and unappealing. Interaction is the spice that creates excitement and interest in e-learning. As with cooking, however, interactivity can be overdone. Too much interaction, like food that is too spicy, results in information overload, or "cognitive indigestion." What might have been an outstanding dish or excellent course becomes unpalatable due to too much of a good thing. Asking learners to respond to four discussion board posts each week, sending several e-mail messages to participants each day, or asking learners to complete three or more online games or activities in a short time leads to "interaction overload." Rather than appreciating the highly interactive learning environment that you have created, trainees will feel bombarded by information and activity and quickly become disenchanted by e-learning. Achieving balance in interactivity is an important goal in e-learning design and delivery.

Successful e-learning programs are those with a balanced blend of interactivity: Learners are confident in their ability to interact with the technology, all systems operate smoothly, content is well developed and organized to maximize learning and motivation, you are involved and available without overpowering the learner, and communication with peers is continuous and engaging. There is no set rule for the amount of interaction appropriate to each of the four levels, rather a function of the complexity of the course and the skill and experience of the trainees. Conducting a thorough needs assessment, including pretesting of learners to address both content knowledge and technology expertise, is the only way to be certain that your course will be challenging but not overwhelming. After the needs assessment, provide just-in-time learner support in the form of a content knowledge base, online manual, help desk, and facilitator guidance so courses can reach an audience with a broader array of skill levels. The type of intervention you choose depends on the results of the needs assessment. Only through careful analysis will you be prepared to address the varying abilities of your audience.

When distance learners lack experience with web-based delivery, you must give more attention to learner-interface to create expertise in the basic functions of the course delivery system. As experience increases, learner-content and learner-learner interactions become primary foci of the course. Trainees engage in frequent and rich peer communication surrounding challenging course content, while your presence and the technology fade. When this transition occurs too quickly and novice learners are immediately thrust into complex content and highly involved peer communication, frustration and overload can result.[15] Trainees may see the endless interactions as meaningless busy work or they may have difficulty connecting content to course goals and objectives. Learners then become overwhelmed by too much too soon, and you find yourself drowning in communication. When your activities are poorly designed or beyond the scope of the learner, you will be required to provide much clarification and massive support. As you design e-learning interaction, remember that frequency does not equal quality.[16]

Changing Roles of Trainers and Learners

As the learning environment changes, so does the role of the key players—you who design and deliver programs and learners who participate in them. As a trainer, you must alter your traditional teaching methods of lectures, discussions, and requiring trainees to internalize facts. Instead, you become a facilitator rather than disseminator of information, and thus focus your attention on creating and facilitating learning experiences that promote the development of implicit knowledge. As a facilitator, you provide the rich environments and learning experiences needed for collaborative study. You act as a "guide by the side" rather than the "sage on stage"—a role that incorporates mediation, modeling, and coaching.

The role of the trainee shifts from that of a passive vessel to be filled with your knowledge to that of an active participant in the learning environment. One important new trainee role is that of explorer. Interaction with the physical world and with other people allows learners to discover concepts and apply skills. Trainees also become teachers themselves by integrating what they have learned and sharing it with others. Hence, they become producers of knowledge, capable of making significant contributions to the organization's knowledge base, creating new and more effective methods of solving key problems. There is a move toward a constructivist approach to e-learning design, where learners interact with content, with each other, and with the instructor to create their own knowledge and meaning.

Constructivist Learning

Constructivism is an educational philosophy founded on the premise that by reflecting on our experiences, we construct our own understanding of the world in which we live. Learning is the process of adjusting our mental models to accommodate new experiences. Learning takes place when we construct and reconstruct knowledge from intellectually engaging experiences and invest in personally meaningful tasks.[17] Knowledge construction will occur more readily when learners are given educational opportunities that integrate thinking, feeling, and acting.[18] Following are its key precepts.

- ◆ *Situated or anchored learning.* This presumes that most learning is context dependent, so that cognitive experiences situated in authentic activities such as project-based learning, cognitive apprenticeships, or case-based learning environments result in richer and more meaningful learning experiences. Contextual instruction creates a necessary link between the classroom and the workplace. Instruction is placed within the environment or context where it will be used with trainees referencing real problems associated with authentic work roles. Contextual learning emphasizes higher level thinking; knowledge transfer; and collecting, analyzing, and synthesizing information and data from multiple sources and viewpoints. When content and context are linked, knowledge is more accessible to learners when new problems arise.[19] Situated or anchored learning presumes that most learning is context dependent, so that cognitive experiences situated in authentic activities result in richer and more meaningful learning experiences.

♦ *Collaborative learning.* This must be a principal focus of learning activities so that negotiation and testing of knowledge can occur.[20] There must be clear, positive interdependence among learners as they seek to achieve a common goal. You must design coursework around the idea of groups of learners working together to solve problems as they develop newer and better ways of getting things done.[21] You must build in opportunities for regular group self-evaluation so learners might master the material and construct knowledge. In addition, you must create courses that provide opportunity to practice small group social skills, fostering the achievement of common goals and promoting interdependence in learning and success.

Papert characterizes behavioral approaches as "clean" teaching, whereas constructivist approaches are "dirty" teaching. Clean training reduces knowledge to formulas describing steps; dirty training is emotional, complex, and intertwined with the learner's social, cultural, and cognitive context.[22] Clean training is based on the premise that trainees are empty vessels to be filled with knowledge by the trainer. In contrast, dirty training proposes that trainees have the ability to construct their own understanding by drawing on their past experiences.

Multiple perspectives, authentic activities, and real-world environments are just some of the themes frequently associated with constructivist learning and teaching. Following is a synthesis of the characteristics of constructivist learning.

♦ Multiple perspectives and representations of concepts and content are presented and encouraged.

♦ Goals and objectives are derived by the trainee or in negotiation with the trainer or system.

♦ Trainers serve in the role of guides, monitors, coaches, tutors, and facilitators.

♦ Activities, opportunities, tools, and environments are provided to encourage metacognition, self-analysis, self-regulation, reflection, and awareness.

♦ The trainee plays a central role in mediating and controlling learning.

♦ Learning situations, environments, skills, content, and tasks are relevant, realistic, authentic, and represent the natural complexities of the real world.

♦ Knowledge construction, not reproduction, is emphasized.

♦ Previous knowledge constructions, beliefs, and attitudes are considered in the knowledge construction process.

♦ Problem solving, higher order thinking skills and deep understanding are emphasized.

♦ Errors provide the opportunity for insight into trainees' previous knowledge constructions.

♦ Exploration is a favored approach in order to encourage trainees to seek knowledge independently and to manage the pursuit of their goals.

- Learners are provided with the opportunity for apprenticeship learning in which there is an increasing complexity of tasks, skills, and knowledge acquisition.
- Collaborative and cooperative learning are favored in order to expose the learner to alternative viewpoints.
- Scaffolding is facilitated to help trainees perform just beyond the limits of their ability.

CHAPTER 3
Constructivist E-Learning Design

When fashioning highly interactive, constructivist learning on the web, you must adopt a strategy based on the course objectives, learner characteristics, environment, and appropriate grounded theory to orchestrate events to sequence interaction. When planning course interaction, it is important to do the following:

1. Identify course goals and objectives.
2. Assess learner preknowledge and characteristics.
3. Build motivational elements.
4. Select a grounded instructional strategy (see Table 3.1 later in the chapter).
5. Define events that will occur at each level of interactivity to facilitate learners' achievement of course objectives.
6. Select appropriate technological delivery tools for each interaction.

The steps provide a sound foundation upon which you may build a highly interactive program that will allow learners to achieve course goals. There is ample space for creativity, excitement, and the development of motivating activities and interactions within this framework. This chapter will examine specific measures you might take to achieve each step.

Step 1: Identify Course Goals and Objectives

Each course must contribute in some way to the achievement of the organization's strategic plan and business goals. Only by conducting a thorough needs assessment will you, the course designer, be able to identify the training goals and objectives that also contribute to the success of the organization as a whole. Once the overarching goals are identified, you must break the learning goal into a subset of smaller tasks or learning objectives. By definition, a behavioral objective should have three components.[23]

1. *Behavior.* The behavior should be specific and observable.
2. *Condition.* The conditions under which the behavior is to be completed should be stated, including what tools or assistance is to be provided.
3. *Standard.* The level of performance that is desirable should be stated, including an acceptable range of answers that are allowable as correct.

Consider the following behavioral objective: *Given an e-learning interface and an established forum, the trainee will be able to post a discussion board thread with 100% accuracy.* This example describes the observable behavior (posting a thread), the conditions (given an e-learning interface and an established forum), and the standard (100% accuracy). Today, the performance objectives in most training programs ignore an indication of the conditions and standards. When these are omitted, it is assumed that the conditions involve normal workplace conditions, and standards are set at perfection. What is always included, however, is the most important criteria for a valuable objective—a written indication of the behavior using measurable or observable verbs. According to Mager,[24] vague verbs such as "understand," "know," or "learn about" should be replaced with more specific verbs. For example, "At the conclusion of this lesson you will be able to . . . (list, identify, state, describe, define, etc.) the course objectives.

Step 2: Assess Learner Preknowledge and Characteristics

Perform an in-depth analysis of your learners and their characteristics to create an interactive environment that meets the needs of your particular audience. At the most basic level, consider the following learner characteristics.[25]

- ◆ *Physical features:* age, gender, disabilities
- ◆ *Education:* fields of study, degrees earned, computer literacy
- ◆ *Cultural background:* language, place of origin, traditions, sensitive subjects
- ◆ *Employment background:* experience, time in current job, relationships with other participants
- ◆ *Expectations:* reasons for attending the course, expected results

The information that you gather from your survey, interview, or focus group will allow you to apply or practice the following options.[26]

Use the Appropriate Language

The reading level, native language, work-based vocabulary, and age of your learners will effect the way you speak to them in your e-learning course. To ensure that you are addressing appropriate language needs as you design your courseware, ask the following questions.

- ◆ Will my audience understand the jargon that I am using?
- ◆ Am I using inclusive gender (he and she)?
- ◆ Will anyone be offended by the words I am using?

Consider Learner Preparation

We often address the prerequisite technology experience that participants must have to be effective, but we must not forget to also address basic course prerequisites. Consider the following questions.

- What is the learner's past experience with course content? Refer to course objectives and pretest knowledge, skills, and abilities.
- Do any participants have specific learning disadvantages that might require additional support or prework?
- Are participants skilled in using the technology and interface of course delivery?
- What range of audience skill can you accommodate in your course?
- How will you handle variation in learner preparedness in your course design?
- How will you deal with learners who are unable to meet course prerequisite skill level?

Adjust Course Pace

You will need to adjust course pace based on the skill, motivation, and time constraints of your audience. Consider the following questions.

- Approximately how much time do trainees have to devote to prework, course delivery, peer communication, and supplemental reading?
- Am I planning for variation in learner skill acquisition? Are there options for fast-track learners and other options for those with learning challenges?
- What is the time frame for the course delivery?

Provide Additional Support

The majority of new e-learners will need additional support from their instructor. Consider the following questions.

- Do participants lack basic job knowledge and skills?
- Are participants experienced in technology?
- Do participants feel unsure or insecure about using the technology of e-learning?

Assess Pretraining Environment and Learner Motivation

Just as many environmental and internal factors can affect traditional training outcomes, so can they inhibit or support online learning. Consider the following questions.

- How was the learner assigned to the course? Was it voluntary or required?
- How does the learner's supervisor support e-learning and the particular program of study?
- How will performance be supported and rewarded back on the job?
- What do participants expect to learn from the course?

Assess Available Technology

Consider the type and level of technology available to trainees at work and at home. Consider the following questions.

- What type of equipment will the trainee have access to at work? At home?
- In addition to the facilitator, will there be a help desk to address problems with technology?

Consider Learner's Capability of Working in Virtual Teams or Groups

Consider the degree of training or expertise the learner has had in group interaction and process. The majority of learners enjoy and benefit from team projects and small group activities.

- Do learners understand guidelines for virtual communication (for example, netiquette)?
- Do learners understand their role as a group member?
- Do they know how to recognize and deal with intergroup conflict?

Step 3: Build Motivational Elements

Motivation is critical to e-learning success. There are many motivating factors in traditional training that cannot be transferred to a virtual environment. For example, would you rather go to the training room, sit with a friend and have a sweet roll while learning about the new inventory system, or stay in your cube and stare at your monitor all afternoon? Motivation in e-learning is critical to the success of the learning experience. Anything you do to motivate your students is beneficial. Do not be afraid to entertain them. Good trainers are expert entertainers.[27] E-learning must be compelling and engaging to keep the learner involved, interested, and stimulated. Learning experiences must be memorable, motivational, and magical if they are to make a lasting impact on learners.[28]

Motivation is defined as the internal processes that give behavior its energy and direction.[29] Motivated behavior originates from needs, cognitions, and emotions, which in turn energize and direct behavior to be initiated, sustained, intensified, or stopped. As an e-learning designer and deliverer, you must create courses that spark the need to learn, provide opportunity for critical thinking and cognition, and generate an emotional response so your learners will be motivated to energize and direct their behavior to meet course objectives. An excellent framework for generating learning motivation is Keller's ARCS model.

ARCS Model of Motivation

The ARCS model of motivational design is a well-known and widely applied system of instructional design. Simple, yet powerful, the ARCS model is rooted in a number of motivational theories and concepts.[30] Keller proposes four conditions that must be met for a learner to be motivated to learn.[31] These are attention strategies, relevance strategies, confidence strategies, and satisfaction strategies.

Attention strategies are used for arousing and sustaining curiosity and interest. They address the following:

◆ *Perceptual arousal:* provides novelty, surprise, incongruity, or uncertainty (Example: The e-learning class opens with an appropriate joke, an arresting theme, or story.)

◆ *Inquiry arousal:* stimulates curiosity by posing questions or problems to solve (Example: The e-learning course opens with a work-based scenario describing a key problem that must be solved during the training program.)

◆ *Variability:* incorporates a range of methods and media to meet learners' varying needs (Example: After displaying and reviewing each process step in a text-based display, ask learners to use mindmapping or concept mapping software to create a graphic representation of the process.)

Relevance strategies link to learners' needs, interests, and motives. They address the following:

◆ *Goal orientation:* presents the objectives, useful purpose of the instruction, and specific methods for successful achievement (Example: The trainer explains the objectives of the lesson and links these to the career-based objectives of the participants.)

◆ *Motive matching:* matches objectives to student needs and motives (Example: The trainer allows students to choose work-based projects that will develop readily transferable skills.)

◆ *Familiarity:* presents content in a manner that is readily understood and also relates to the learners' experiences and values (Example: The trainer asks the learners to provide problem examples from their own experiences in discussion board posts.)

Confidence strategies help students develop positive expectation for successful achievement. They address the following:

◆ *Learning requirements:* inform trainees of performance requirements and assessment criteria (Example: The trainer provides participants with a rubric and examples of past projects.)

◆ *Success opportunities:* provide challenging and meaningful opportunities for successful learning (Example: The designer uses an intelligent tutor or knowledge base to provide support and quick answers to relevant questions.)

◆ *Personal responsibility:* links learning success to students' personal effort and ability (Example: Trainees create learning contracts that are frequently updated and assessed throughout the course.)

Satisfaction strategies provide extrinsic and intrinsic reinforcement for effort. They include the following:

◆ *Intrinsic reinforcement:* encourages and supports intrinsic enjoyment of the learning experience (Example: The trainer links course objectives to individual learners' career objectives.)

♦ *Extrinsic rewards:* provides positive reinforcement and motivational feedback (Example: The trainer provides awards to students for outstanding work and holds a virtual awards ceremony in a synchronous environment to give recognition.)

♦ *Equity:* maintains consistent standards and consequences for success (Example: Provide frequent feedback in an objective manner to each trainee individually throughout the course.)

The ARCS model will support the development of interesting and motivating e-learning courses. Its simplicity and clarity make it one of the most elegant theories of instruction, and certainly deserving of your attention

Step 4: Select a Grounded Instructional Strategy

Of the many instructional theories that might guide e-learning development, some lend themselves more readily to the development of interactivity than others. The application of a grounded instructional theory gives you a foundation for creating and facilitating online interaction. Without such a basis, interactions will be little more than busywork with few links to course objectives and sound learning practice. Table 3.1 contains examples of theories grounded in academic study and research. To create rich interaction, consider theories that not only address the organization of content, but also user participation and motivation. Two excellent theories that lend themselves to the design of interactive e-learning are Keller's ARCS model and Gagne's nine events of instruction. You reviewed the ARCS model in the previous section as a motivational structure. Now you will examine Gagne's nine events as a design model.

Gagne's Nine Events of Instruction

In his book, *The Conditions of Learning,* Gagne outlines nine instructional events and their corresponding cognitive processes.[32]

1. *Gain attention.* Learning begins with the capturing of the learner's attention. Curiosity can be aroused by using a picture, paradox, thought-provoking question, analogy, or anecdote. You might also add a little flair early on in the form of sound effects, an animated title screen, or a video clip.
2. *Inform learners of objectives.* Stating objectives and revisiting them later in the course will let trainees know what they will learn and how it will be measured.
3. *Stimulate recall of prior learning.* Associating new information with prior knowledge can facilitate the learning process. Links to previous knowledge facilitate the storage of new knowledge in long-term memory. An advance or-

ganizer or a forum that queries previous experience will facilitate recall of past knowledge.

4. *Present the content.* Provide efficiently organized information using appropriate text, graphics, and media that communicate the message effectively. Content should be chunked and organized meaningfully. Typically, processes are explained and then demonstrated. A variety of media should be used when possible, including graphic organizers, audio, and video. Consider novel ways to present content by embedding it in a theme-based course or by using an overarching scenario.

5. *Provide "learning guidance."* To facilitate the encoding of information in long-term memory, provide an array of guidance strategies. Consider accelerated learning principles and include graphics, mnemonics, stories, analogies, and pictures. In addition, provide a knowledge base and expert support to facilitate research and independent study for project work.

6. *Elicit performance (practice).* In this event of instruction, the learner is required to practice or demonstrate the new skill or behavior. Performance might take place through the posting of project work on the discussion board, the development of a web-based presentation, or practice experiences completed outside the e-learning class.

7. *Provide feedback.* As learners practice new behavior, it is important that they receive specific and immediate feedback regarding their performance. Feedback might be formative in nature, allowing for additional work in revision and subsequent demonstration. Feedback may come from peers, you as course facilitator, or external mentors.

8. *Assess performance.* An objective method of assessing performance is administered at the end of the course. This might involve an online test, carefully graded project work, or demonstration of a mastered skill that is evaluated in an unbiased manner.

9. *Enhance retention and transfer to the job.* Testing, surveys, and interviews are conducted at regular intervals following course completion to assess transfer. Technology can facilitate transfer by allowing learners to stay connected after the training experience. Discussion groups can remain intact and continue to share posttraining experiences and knowledge. Regular virtual communication with employees and their supervisor can enhance on-the-job practice. In addition, course updates and future revision can be readily passed on to trainees through the electronic delivery of minicourses and newsbriefs.

Table 3.2 shows how you might sequence e-learning events using Gagne's theory. The first column lists the nine events of instruction, the center column contains a brief explanation, and the end column lists interactive strategies, many included in this textbook, that will help you create the nine events in your courses.

Table 3.1
Summary of Instructional Strategies for E-Learning

Keller's ARCS Model[1]	Gagne's Nine Events[2]	Goal-Based Scenarios[3]	Anchored Instruction[4]
Attention • Perceptual arousal • Inquiry arousal • Variability **Relevance** • Goal orientation • Motive matching • Familiarity **Confidence** • Learning requirements • Success opportunities • Personal responsibility **Satisfaction** • Instrinsic reinforcement • Extrinsic rewards • Equity	1. Gain attention 2. Inform learners of objectives 3. Recall prior knowledge 4. Present material 5. Provide guided learning 6. Elicit performance 7. Provide feedback 8. Assess performance 9. Enhance retention and transfer	**Mission** refers to the primary goal that the student pursues within the goal-based scenario. **Mission foci** may be of different orientations, including design, discovery, exploration, and control. **Cover story** refers to the premise, designed by the instructor, under which the mission will be pursued. **Scenario operations** refer to the specific activities that the student performs in pursuit of a mission.	1. Learning and teaching activities are designed around an "anchor" which is based on a case study or problem. 2. Curriculum materials should allow exploration by the learner. 3. Learners take ownership of learning process. 4. Involves complex content, solved through interconnectedness of subproblems, multiple scenarios presented. 5. Problem is presented in a narrative format or story with embedded data. 6. Learning context is generative (students identify; become actively involved in generating solution).

Simulation Model[5]	Experiential Learning Model[6]	Constructivist Learning[7]	Problem-Based Learning[8]

1. **Orientation**
  • Present broad topic of simulation and major concepts.
  • Explain simulation and gaming.
  • Give overview of the simulation.
2. **Participant training**
  • Set up scenario.
  • Assign roles.
  • Hold abbreviated practice session.
	Experience—Immerse learner in "authentic" experience (e.g., real or simulated job task). Learners generate individual information using applicable senses.
	
	Publish—Talking or writing about experience. Sharing observations, thoughts, and feelings.
	
	Process—Debrief: Interpret published information, defining patterns, discrepancies, and overall dynamics; making sense of the information generated.
		Knowledge construction: Provide experience with knowledge construction process.
		
		Multiple perspectives: Provide experience in and appreciation for multiple perspectives.
		
		Authentic: Embed learning in realistic and relevant context.
		
		Voice: Encourage ownership and voice in learning process.
		
		Social: Embed learning in social experience.
			1. Start new class
			  • Introductions
			  • Climate setting (including teacher/tutor role)
			  • Start new problem
			  • Set problem
			  • Bring problem home
			  • Describe the product/performance required
			  • Assign tasks
			  • Reason through the problem (i.e., ideas/hypotheses, facts, learning issues, and action plan)

3. **Simulation operations**
   • Conduct game activity and game administration.
   • Give feedback and evaluation.
   • Clarify misconceptions.
   • Continue simulation.
4. **Participant debriefing**
   • Summarize events and perceptions.
   • Summarize insights.
   • Analyze process.
   • Compare simulation activity to the real world.
   • Appraise and redesign the simulation.

Internalize—Private, learner reflects on lessons learned, means of managing conflicting data, and requirements for future learning.

Generalize—Develop hypotheses, form generalizations, and reach conclusions from information and knowledge gained from lesson.

Apply—Use knowledge gained from lesson to make decisions and solve problems. Put learned skills and knowledge into action.

Multimedia: Encourage use of multiple modes of representation.

Reflection: Encourage self-awareness of knowledge construction process.

   • Commitment as to probable outcome
   • Learning issues shaping/assignment
   • Resource identification
   • Schedule follow-up
2. Problem follow-up
   • Resources used and their critique
   • Reassess problem
3. Performance presentation
4. After conclusion of problem
   • Knowledge abstraction and summary
   • Self-evaluations

[1] J. M. Keller, "Motivational design of instruction," in C. M. Reigeluth (Ed.), *Instructional Design Theories and Models: An Overview of Their Current Status* (Hillsdale, NJ: Erlbaum, 1983).

[2] R. Gagne, *The Conditions of Learning* (4th ed.) (New York: Holt, Rinehart & Winston, 1985).

[3] R. C. Schank, A. Fano, B. Bell, & M. Jona, "The design of goal-based scenarios," *The Journal of the Learning Sciences* 3 (1993/1994): 305–345.

[4] J. D. Bransford, "Anchored instruction: Why we need it and how technology can help," in D. Nix & R. Sprio (Eds.), *Cognition, Education and Multimedia* (Hillsdale, NJ: Erlbaum Associates, 1990).

[5] B. Joyce, M. Weil, & B. Showers, *Models of Teaching* (4th ed.) (Needham Heights, MA: Allyn and Bacon, 1992).

[6] J. W. Pfeiffer & J. E. Jones "Introduction to the structured experiences section," in J.E. Jones & J.W. Pfeiffer (Eds.), *The 1975 Annual Handbook for Group Facilitators* (La Jolla, CA: University Associates, 1975).

[7] P. C. Honebein, "Seven goals for the design of constructivist learning environments," in B. Wilson (Ed.), *Constructivist Learning Environments: Case Studies in Instructional Design* (Englewood Cliffs, NJ: Educational Technology Publications, 1996), 3–8.

[8] H. S. Barrows, *How to Design a Problem Based Curriculum for the Preclinical Years* (New York: Springer Publishing Co., 1985).

Table 3.2

Designing and Sequencing E-Learning Interactivity Using Gagne's Nine Events[1]

Event	How to Elicit	Examples
1. Gain attention	Create novelty, uncertainty, or surprise	• Send invitation to learn[*] • Open with overarching scenario[*] • Create a course theme • Use pedagogical agent • Add audio clip to start • Use icebreakers[*]
2. Inform learners of objectives	Describe criteria for performance and involve learners in goal setting	• Include course objectives • Use learning contracts • Create course goals forum • Include rubrics and sample projects
3. Stimulate recall of prior knowledge	Learners identify and share prior knowledge and experience	• Storytelling forum[*] • What I Know for Sure[*] • Virtual interview[*] • Mindmap of current knowledge[*] • Pretest
4. Present content	Provide course content	• Knowledge base • Web resources • Textbook • PowerPoint slides
5. Provide learning guidance	Facilitate learner understanding of content	• Dear Abby[*] • FAQ forum • Mindmaps[*] • Graphics • Job aids • Peer learning activities[*]
6. Elicit performance	Learners demonstrate new understanding	• Scenario learning assignment[*] • Content review and practice[*] • Group discussion[*]
7. Provide feedback	Tell learners how they are doing	• Instructor feedback • Peer review • Self-review • External review
8. Assess performance	Determine whether learner achieved the objectives	• Assessment checklist • Assessment rubric • Learner portfolio
9. Enhance retention and transfer	Facilitate learner retention and application of new knowledge	• Content practice and review[*] • E-mail check-up[*]

[*]Learn more about these activities in the chapters that follow.
[1]R. Gagne, *The Conditions of Learning* (4th ed.) (New York: Holt, Rinehart & Winston, 1985).

Step 5: Define Events

Applying Gagne's nine-step model or Keller's ARCS model to e-learning design will go far to ensure the development of sound training programs. You might apply the theories separately, or combine both models. Table 3.3 contains a matrix that will help you to visualize the enactment of key learning events at each of the four levels of interactivity. In the appropriate boxes, you may list the specific level of interaction as it pertains to each event. By doing so, you will create balanced interactivity by applying Gagne's nine events to your design. Table 3.4 contains a sample matrix that includes plans for interactive e-learning exercises from this textbook. Shorter, more focused courses might not require all four levels of interaction at each step, but the sample matrix allows you to see how the activities here can be used to plan a highly interactive course.

Table 3.3

Interactive E-Learning Design

Combine Gagne's nine events[1] with the four levels of interaction to plan e-learning.

Gagne's Nine Events	Levels of Interaction			
	Learner-Interface	Learner-Content	Learner-Facilitation	Learner-Learner
1. Gain attention				
2. Inform learner of objectives				
3. Recall prior knowledge				
4. Present material				
5. Provide guided learning				
6. Elicit performance				
7. Provide feedback				
8. Assess performance				
9. Enhance retention and transfer				

[1] R. Gagne, *The Conditions of Learning* (4th ed.) (New York: Holt, Rinehart & Winston, 1985).

Step 6: Select Appropriate Technological Delivery Tools

Next you must determine how you will deliver the course to your learners. The type of technological resources you have available will determine your method of delivery. At the most basic level, your first decision is whether to offer the course synchronously or asynchronously.

Table 3.4
Interactive E-Learning Design Sample

Combine Gagne's Nine Events[1] with the four levels of interaction to plan e-learning.

Gagne's Nine Events	Levels of Interaction			
	Learner-Interface	Learner-Content	Learner-Facilitation	Learner-Learner
1. Gain attention	Audio/video clip	Overarching theme	Invitation to learn	Icebreaker
2. Inform learner of objectives	Technology requirements	Goal-based scenario/problem-based learning	Course objectives	Team icebreaker
3. Recall prior knowledge	Technology skill quiz	Mindmap	E-mail game	Brainwriting
4. Present material	Text, audio, video delivery	Content review & practice activities	Respond to questions, office hours	Content-based group discussion
5. Provide guided learning	Electronic guide, help desk, knowledge base	Content review & practice activities	Respond to questions, office hours	Peer learning activities
6. Elicit performance	Quizzes	Major project presentation	Online role play	Group discussion exercise
7. Provide feedback	Quiz results/grades	Compare work to sample projects	Personal e-mail	Peer feedback/electronic yearbook
8. Assess performance	Quiz results/grades	Compare performance to rubric & objectives	Compare performance to rubric & objectives	Peer feedback/virtual cruise
9. Enhance retention and transfer	Final exam	Content review & practice activities	E-mail check-up	Virtual reunion

[1] R. Gagne, *The Conditions of Learning* (4th ed.) (New York: Holt, Rinehart & Winston, 1985).

Asynchronous Delivery

Asynchronous communication allows you to move beyond the confines of scheduling so you and your learners may interact within the course and with materials at their convenience. Communication does not take place in real time, allowing maximum flexibility and freedom of use. Added benefits are learners have time to research and reflect upon their responses, and global communication is possible without time zone constraint. Challenges that must be addressed in asynchronous training relate to the self-directed nature of the learning experience. Without opportunity to connect with both the facilitator and other learners, asynchronous training leads to isolation, apathy, and eventual disenchantment with the learning mode. When the designer and facilitator attend to the need for interaction in both the planning and delivery stage, this weakness in asynchronous learning can be overcome, allowing its users to reap the many benefits of on-demand training. The following tools will help you deliver your course asynchronously.

E-mail

E-mail is the most commonly used collaborative tool, particularly for private one-to-one communications. It can be a useful tool for collaborative and project-based learning activities.

Discussion Forums

Discussion forums are online tools that capture the exchange of messages over time, sometimes over a period of days, weeks, or months. Threaded discussion forums are organized into categories so that the exchange of messages and responses is grouped and easy to find. Discussion forum tools are similar to newsgroups or bulletin board systems, where text conversations taking place over time are displayed. The organization of the messages can be a simple temporal sequence or the messages can be presented as a threaded discussion where only those on a specific topic or thread are displayed in sequence.

Threaded Discussion

Threaded discussion is an online dialogue or conversation that takes the form of a series of linked messages. The series is created over time as users read and reply to existing messages. Typically, messages in a given thread share a common subject line and are linked to each other in the order of their creation. Without threaded discussion, the reader would confront a chaotic, unsorted list of messages on varied topics. By hyperlinking messages that share a common subject line, threaded discussion makes it convenient for the reader to focus on one conversation and avoid the distractions of unrelated postings.

Online Journals

Online journals enable learners to make notes in a personal or private journal. They can share these journal entries with you or other learners, but cannot share private journal entries. This tool can be used to facilitate writing assignments where parts are written over time and then later assembled into a document. This tool also can be used to make personal annotations to pages of a course that can later be used as a study aide. The Online Notes tool can also record reflections about personal learning accomplishments.

MUDs/MOOs

MUDs/MOOs are similar to internet relay chat but are asynchronous and have enhanced control and object-oriented features. A MUD (multiuser dungeon, dimension, or domain) is a computer program that users can join and explore. MUDs and MOOs (object-oriented MUDs) have been used in educational settings and evolved from the game Dungeons & Dragons. Original systems use only text but allow user control over various features. Graphical systems exist but interaction is still text based. Although the use of MUDs and MOOs can be difficult to create and use, take a look at the "Mini Moo" exercise in Chapter 5. It can add the flavor of role playing without the complications of a full-scale MOO.

Synchronous Delivery

Synchronous e-learning requires that all parties be online simultaneously. The convenience that synchronous training offers over traditional delivery is the time saved in travel. Synchronous interaction allows for immediate feedback and enhanced social interaction. It more accurately approximates communication in the classroom where time restraints govern the frequency and length of interaction. The disadvantages of synchronous training include occasional technical difficulties that cause communication outages, scheduling difficulties that occur when all parties must be at their computers and ready to learn simultaneously, and the need to limit class size to allow the facilitator to adequately address individual learners. Following are common tools used in synchronous courses.

Internet Relay Chat

Internet relay chat, or chat for short, allows "live" public one-to-one and one-to-many interactions. Live text interaction occurs in real time, which is limiting for those with busy schedules, but motivating and fun for those eager to communicate with people online. Chat can allow learners to read and share more information than a regular classroom discussion. We speak at approximately 120 words per minute, and only one person can effectively speak at a time. Classroom discussions are limited to participants in the class and onsite visitors. Because more than one learner can type at a time and we can read 400 to 1,000 words per minute, the class can be exposed to more information in the same amount of time. Finally, transcripts of the chat sessions can be saved or printed so that learners do not have to scramble to take notes.

Desktop Videoconferencing

Desktop videoconferencing allows "live" one-to-one or one-to-several video interactions. Using a color video camera, free software, a computer, and an internet connection, you can have color, two-way video with audio of a quality dependent on your bandwidth. Desktop video depends on the speed of your internet access. Motion may be jerky, causing distracting facial distortions as the video frame freezes intermittently, and the audio may be raspy and difficult to hear.

Whiteboards

Whiteboards function as graphical chat tools. They allow multiple users to draw, paint, and share existing graphical files in real time. Whiteboards typically contain some combination of the following tools: pencil, eraser, text, color, lines, and various shapes. Each vendor offers different whiteboard features, such as the capability to import files and use them in the style of prepared flip charts. Some have the capability for multiple people to write on the whiteboard simultaneously. For visual learners, a whiteboard can be an effective tool in the synchronous classroom. Whiteboards allow for instant visual communication over a long distance and invite everyone to participate. Of course, there are space limitations to the use of the whiteboard, but the ability to graphically represent ideas in real time, albeit in a smaller venue than the trusty classroom blackboards, offers the advantage of engaging learners visually.

Instant Messaging

Instant messaging (sometimes called IM or IMing) is the ability to easily see if chosen friends or co-workers are connected to the internet and to exchange messages with them. Instant messaging differs from ordinary e-mail in the immediacy of the message exchange and also makes a continued exchange simpler than sending e-mail back and forth. Most exchanges are text only; however, some services allow attachments. In order for IMing to work, users must subscribe to the service, be online at the same time, and the intended recipient must be willing to accept instant messages.

The majority of the games and exercises in this textbook can be delivered synchronously or asynchronously, depending on time allowances and the needs of your learners. Synchronous games and activities are quick paced and can be completed in a short time. The challenge is to get everyone together online to participate. Asynchronous games can take extra time as progress depends on participants' frequent attention to the forum.

Delivery Media

Your next decision is to determine the media that you will use to deliver your course. Options include text based, audio, video, and graphic media, or a combination of the four.

Text-based Delivery

Text-based delivery has the lowest technology, and is the least expensive medium. It involves delivering content and assignments via print media that learners view on the computer and print out. Text has some advantages: Files are small and perform well at low bandwidth, users can search for specific words or phrases, and content can be updated easily. Text is not limited to on-screen delivery, but can include books, manuals, print-based readings, and reference materials. Many online learners benefit from a hard copy of the course content, eliminating the need for printing screens.

Graphics

Graphics enhance online training and can include photographs, screenshots, illustrations, and flowcharts. Most web browsers can display .gif and .jpeg files, which are bitmap files of relatively small size. Techniques for optimizing graphics so they load more quickly include decreasing the resolution, size, and number of colors. Use graphic editing software (Adobe, Macromedia) to optimize your graphics and to convert nondigital components to digital files. These can then be easily added to your course content to add visual appeal to a text-based delivery.

Animation

Animation illustrates concepts with movement, shows processes, or draws attention to a region or elements of a screen. Although development time can be quite lengthy, animation can add effective teaching components to skills-based courses.

Audio

Audio can enhance learning concepts and reinforce ideas presented as text or graphics. Three types of audio commonly used are music, narration voice-overs, and sound effects. Using a streaming format to deliver files allows them to start playing before the entire audio file has been downloaded.

Video

Video requires high bandwidth to download but it is useful for conveying visual information and adding a sense of realism to courseware. Video is captured, edited, and optimized in video editors. If video is too bandwidth intensive, substitute still graphics, audio, or animation to make downloading more efficient.

Interactive Approaches

The exercises and activities that follow will allow you to create interactive e-learning courses that facilitate constructivist learning. They are divided into categories pertaining to their purpose.

- ◆ Session openers or icebreakers
- ◆ Scenario learning activities
- ◆ Peer learning

- Content review and practice
- Group discussion
- Idea generation
- Closers

Most contain prewritten instructions that you may incorporate in your e-learning course. As with all suggestions in this textbook, you must use your own knowledge of your learners and their needs to guide you in selecting and delivering learning activities.

CHAPTER 4
Session Openers

Session openers or icebreakers are brief activities that set the tone for the course. They send learners the message that participation is valued, that relationships with classmates are important, and that this course will be interesting and interactive. Icebreakers provide e-learners with an opportunity to connect with their classmates and interact with new technology. Without this initial connection, e-learners might feel lost in cyberspace. These activities also serve to set learner expectations for the course. Let trainees know from the start that their interaction with you and other classmates is important. The structured introductions and prework that take place in session openers accelerate openness, sharing, and collaborative learning later in the course. Use e-learning session openers to do the following:

◆ Introduce learners to their classmates and help them develop positive relationships. Create a sound foundation that will benefit learners later when they collaborate in team projects, group discussion, and peer learning activities.

◆ Make a positive first impression and set course expectations. Interesting session openers set a positive, fun, interactive tone for the course from the start. Learners' interest is piqued and they are motivated to explore the course.

◆ Facilitate confidence in using new technology. Opening activities require learners to use technology without the added burden of working with course content. Learners develop comfort and confidence in navigating the course site, posting to the discussion board, and navigating the web as they complete session openers. Later, students will utilize these skills as they progress through the course.

Electronic Business Card

Overview	Learners create and distribute electronic business cards to introduce themselves and communicate their online identity.
Objective	Design an electronic business card that communicates each learner's virtual identity and use the card for class introductions.
Resources	None necessary
Delivery	Asynchronous delivery via discussion board forum
Process	Learners create virtual business cards and post them to a discussion board forum so they can introduce themselves to classmates. Provide the following instructions:

> *Business cards are an important part of our workplace identity. Because we are meeting virtually, we cannot exchange cards, shake hands, and go through traditional meet-and-greet activities; but we can exchange "virtual business cards" by posting them in a discussion board forum. First, create your card. It should contain a few simple text lines that tell us your name, title, employer, e-mail address, and a brief statement about your particular expertise. For example, John Doe, Lead Trainer, XYZ Corporation, jdoe@xyz.com, "e-learning delivery expert." If time and resources allow, you can create a graphic card, but remember, text is fine. When your card is completed, post the text or link the graphic file to the discussion board forum. Look over the cards of fellow classmates and add appropriate introductory marks to their e-cards.*

Evaluation	Recognize learners for the detail provided in their e-cards and the introductory remarks added to the forum.
Variations	Have learners add photos to their e-cards so that they can connect a name with a face.

First Job

Overview	This icebreaker enables learners to share details about their first job.
Objective	Learners get to know each other and look for common experiences by sharing information about their first job.
Resources	None necessary
Delivery	Asynchronous discussion board forum
Process	Create a discussion board forum that asks learner to:

Tell us about your first job, other than babysitting. Where did you work? What did you do? What did you learn from this experience? Add links that relate to your first job.

Evaluation	No evaluation is necessary, but recognize learners for sharing past experiences.
Variations	After learners have shared their first job experience, follow up with a second post that asks:

How did your first job lead you to what you are doing today? How did this first experience affect your future career?

In a course that addresses career issues, ask learners to continue the assignment and create a timeline that depicts their career experiences, starting with their first job and ending with their current position.

An Invitation to Learn

Overview	Learners receive a formal invitation to attend an e-learning training program.
Objective	Facilitate learner involvement and initiate e-learning by sending a formal invitation to attend the program.
Resources	Using e-mail and optional online greeting card software, create either a letter of invitation or a graphic card inviting learners to the e-learning program.
Delivery	E-mail
Process	Make your initial contact with learners personal and inviting. E-mail either a letter or card inviting each member of your class to participate in the upcoming program. In your card or letter, describe the objectives of the course, details about e-learning, and benefits for the learner.
Evaluation	None necessary
Variations	Ask learners to RSVP by responding to your e-mail and indicating their particular goals for the course.

The Personal Blog

Overview	In this icebreaker, learners create and maintain a personal weblog that describes their background and contains their thoughts, ideas, views, and a chronicle of everyday events.
Objective	Learners create a personal weblog that is made available to their classmates in which they share information about themselves and their ideas, interests, and favorite links.
Resources	Weblog host (see software references for ideas)
Delivery	Place instructions in the course assignments section. Create a discussion board forum to house links to learner weblog sites.
Process	Short for weblog, a *blog* is an online journal that is organized chronologically. Its free-form interface combined with absolute ease of use makes it popular with both experienced web users and novices. Essentially, the blog is a web page that can be updated instantly by the user, and followers can respond with their comments just as quickly. The personal blog provides information about this "blogger," with thoughts, ideas, and opinions, and links to valuable sites and resources. It is an excellent way for your learners to get acquainted with each other and with the web.

Post the following instructions in the assignment section:

Here is your chance to develop your own personal presence on the web by creating a blog. The personal blog, or weblog, is a simple but powerful type of online journal or chronicle that contains links, stories, and your commentary about topics that are important to you (instructor adds links to examples of personal blogs). *It is easy to design and maintain, because new items go on the top and flow down to previous content. Here you will create a personal blog that tells us who you are and what interests you. Here is how to get started: Use a free blog hosting service* (insert links to free sites) *and follow the directions to develop your site. First, briefly tell us about you (career, family, hobbies, travel, etc.). Next, conduct some internet research to identify exciting websites, portals, and articles that you find particularly interesting. Add links to these sites and a brief description, and remember to include your commentary. Once your blog is up and running, go to the discussion board forum and add a thread to post the URL for your blog so your fellow classmates can visit and learn more about you. Be sure to update your blog weekly to add additional links and commentary. Beware, blogging is addictive!*

Note: Create a discussion board forum where learners can post URLs for their blogs. You may also want to encourage (or assign) learners to visit the blogs of fellow classmates and add their comments.

Evaluation	Recognize learners for the detail they provide in the blogs, quality of their links, value and insight of their commentary, and for visiting and actively participating in the blogs of their classmates.
Variations	Blogs can be time consuming to create and maintain. As a variation you may want to place a time limit on the assignment. For example, limit the assignment to a one- or two-week period so learners will not be required to continue their blog throughout the course. Based on the wealth of information provided by your class members' blogs, you can create additional icebreakers. You might create a quiz format, where learners match names to facts or characteristics found in the blogs. You might also have learners search their classmates' blogs to locate the names of those who have certain interests or characteristics, similar to the popular bingo icebreaker.

Blogging Guide

◆ Get to the point.
◆ Express one thought at a time.
◆ Go easy on technical jargon.
◆ Back up claims with references.
◆ Add links to your blog.
◆ Be politically correct and respectful.

Picture This!

Overview	This icebreaker allows participants to share and explain their favorite pictures.
Objective	Participants create a visual connection with the class and also practice their skill in graphic communication.
Resources	Electronic photo files created using a scanner or digital camera
Delivery	Asynchronous discussion board forum
Process	Ask everyone in the group to share a favorite photo with the class by posting it to the discussion board. Provide the following instructions:

Locate a favorite photo and have it transferred to an electronic file (.jpeg or .gif). You can do this by using a scanning device (home, work, local photo shop or copy shop) or by taking the picture to a local photo shop and asking them to create a digital file for you on a floppy disk. Next, go to the forum and create a thread where you tell us a bit about the photo and why it is your favorite. Attach the photo to your message. (Provide directions specific to your platform.) Then view the photos and messages of fellow learners.

Note: You may also ask learners to send you their pictures and create a collage of photos that is added to your course. Learners can then add their explanations of the photos in a separate discussion board forum.

Evaluation	There is no need to evaluate the pictures.
Variations	Instead of favorite photos, you might ask learners to post a current photo of themselves with their bio.

$100,000 Shopping Spree

Overview	This icebreaker and values clarification exercise helps trainees participate in an online spending spree.
Objective	Users on the web are accustomed to anonymously browsing with unprotected privacy. In this exercise, students will break through the anonymity barrier. Learners get to know each other and evaluate their priorities by "spending" $100,000 on anything they would like to purchase via the web. By the end of the activity, learners will feel secure in revealing more information about themselves, leading to a greater degree of trust.
Resources	None necessary
Delivery	Asynchronous discussion board forum
Process	Learners imagine that they have been given $100,000 to spend on the web. What would they buy? What do their purchase decisions say about their values?

Post the following instructions in a discussion board forum:

Imagine that you have been given $100,000 and can spend it on anything that can be purchased online. Add a thread to this forum to tell us how you would spend your money. Provide links to sites for the specific items you would buy. Come as close as possible to spending the entire $100,000.

Next, after all the learners have posted their purchases, follow up with a second forum:

Now that you have spent your money, what do your choices tell us about what is important to you? How does your spending reflect your values?

Evaluation	No evaluation is needed for the first forum, but recognize learners who provide insight into the way their spending reflects their values.
Variations	Prior to the exercise, ask learners to list in order the three things that are most important to them. Do not connect the two exercises initially, but later, after the money has been spent, ask learners how closely their spending habits correlated with their three priorities.

Stupid Technology Questions

Overview	This icebreaker invites learners to create and post "stupid" technology questions.[33]
Objective	By creating "stupid" questions about technology, learners become more comfortable with the questioning process and less self-conscious about asking questions.
Resources	List of opening "Stupid Technology Questions"
Delivery	Asynchronous discussion board forum
Process	Create a discussion board forum with the following instructions:

> *We all know that there is no such thing as a "dumb" question. To help you feel comfortable with asking questions, particularly those about technology, we are going to create a list of "Stupid Technology Questions." To get things started, here are a few tech questions I have been asked:*
> ◆ *Will my laptop work if I don't sit it on my lap?*
> ◆ *What if my floppy disk isn't floppy?*
> ◆ *When it says "click the right mouse button," do they mean my right or theirs?*
> ◆ *Does e-mail get delivered on holidays?*
> ◆ *Why are all websites made by "Dot Com"?*
>   *Add to this list by creating a thread to post one or more additional "stupid" tech questions.*

Evaluation	Recognize learners who post the funniest or most ridiculous questions.
Variations	If your learners are novices to technology and might not actually know the answers to some of the questions, ask them to not only post their questions, but also include what they would say in answer.

Super Sleuths

Overview	This "get to know you" activity involves critical thinking and deduction.
Objective	Learners acquire information about classmates by matching facts from an anonymous post to the appropriate member.
Resources	Create a forum in the discussion board that instructs learners to post details about themselves anonymously, then read the posts of others and match the information with the class member.
Delivery	Asynchronous forum that is delivered in the general discussion board or in group discussion areas
Process	Post the following instructions in your discussion board:

> *Become a super sleuth by matching background information to the correct learner. Start by providing some information about yourself:*
> ◆ *Favorite song*
> ◆ *Favorite place to go with family/friends*
> ◆ *Favorite restaurant*
> ◆ *Favorite movie*
> ◆ *Favorite musician*
> ◆ *Favorite TV show*
> ◆ *Where you were born*
> ◆ *Place you would like to visit on your next vacation*
> ◆ *Goals for this course*
>   *Just this once, make your post anonymously, without including your name in the subject line. Also be sure to check the Anonymous box below. Later, read the posts of all your classmates and match the members' names to the posts. To do this, read each post and click on the Reply button to add a thread. Then write in the message box, "I think this is a description of (group member's name). This guess was made by (your name)," and click Submit. When all the guesses are in, we will tally them and find out who was most successful.*

Evaluation	Give learners a specific due date when all guesses must be in and then tally the correct answers. Recognize those who made the most correct matches and also those learners who were the most difficult to identify.
Variations	In addition to asking learners to identify the source of the anonymous post, ask them to tell why they chose that particular person. This might also lead to a discussion of stereotyping, for example, assuming that male rather than female classmates would prefer rock music or sports.

Two Truths and a Lie

Overview	This introductory activity asks learners to first provide three pieces of information about themselves—two that are true and one that is not—and then class members guess the false statement.
Objective	Have fun while learning more about fellow classmates and detecting potential stereotypes regarding expected characteristics.
Resources	None necessary
Delivery	Asynchronous discussion board forum
Process	This is a great second icebreaker, following a more traditional "tell us about you" post. This way, learners will have information about each other to use as they make their guesses. Create a forum in the discussion board that instructs learners to:
	Please post three details about yourself—two that are true, one that is a lie. Next, read the posts of others that contain their truths and lie and add a thread to their post to guess which statement is the lie. Note that one of the goals of the exercise is to attempt to fool your fellow classmates when they attempt to identify the lie.
Evaluation	Tally the correct answers and recognize the students who made the most correct guesses and also those who created lies that were the most difficult to identify.
Variations	Instead of two general truths and a lie, have learners post two exciting experiences they have actually had plus one that they would like to have in the future. Classmates then guess which two experiences are real and which one is false. Other variations include two goals that have been achieved and a future goal, two jobs that learners have held and one that they want but have not actually held, and so forth.

Virtual Interview

Overview	This icebreaker asks learners to take turns interviewing each other either by e-mail or in a live chat.
Objective	Learners formulate a series of open-ended questions and use reflective listening to draw ideas and information from a partner.
Resources	List of possible open-ended interview questions (see list on page 58).
Delivery	Asynchronous delivery via e-mail or synchronous delivery via live chat or instant messaging
Process	Pair learners with another classmate by posting a list of paired partners in the class assignment section. Instruct learners to make arrangements to meet either live (instant message or private chat) or asynchronously through e-mail to interview each other. Provide the following instructions:

> *In this icebreaker, you will interview a classmate virtually to learn as much about that person as possible. Using the list of suggested interview questions that has been prepared, partner 1 interviews partner 2, using reflecting and restatement to further draw out the interviewee. When you are finished, summarize and post the interview results as a thread in the discussion board. Next, change roles and partner 2 interviews partner 1, posting the results.*

Create a discussion board forum where partners can post the results of their interviews.

Evaluation	Examine the posted results for depth and quality of interaction. Did the interview reveal only a few superficial facts, or was deeper learning and understanding revealed?
Variations	From the postings, you will have a lengthy forum that supplies detailed information about your class. Expand on this exercise by developing a quiz based on the content of the postings that asks learners to match facts or characteristics (loves animals, marathon runner, etc.) with the correct learner.

Virtual Interview Questions

- Tell me a little bit about yourself.
- Why did you decide to take this course?
- What do you enjoy doing in your free time?
- What is your all-time favorite meal?
- Who was the best teacher you ever had? What made that teacher so great?
- What do you most enjoy about your present job?
- What one talent or gift would you really like to have?
- If you could choose to have any job in the world—other than the one you have right now—what would it be? Why?
- If you could have dinner with anyone in the world, who would you choose?

What I Know for Sure

Overview	This icebreaker asks learners to describe what they "know for sure" about the topic of study.
Objective	Recall and construct knowledge of the topic of study.
Resources	None necessary
Delivery	Asynchronous discussion board forum
Process	Provide the following instructions:

> *As Oprah fans know, the maven of daytime talk ends her magazine, O, with a column entitled, "What I Know for Sure." Tell us what you know for sure about* (course topic). *To do this, go to the discussion board forum and add a thread where you tell us two or more things you "know for sure" or at least for "pretty sure" about* (topic).

Evaluation	Review the topics to get a feel for the depth of knowledge held by your class. Recognize learners for detailed answers and the expertise they bring to your class.
Variations	Ask learners to revisit their post at the end of the course and add to their "know for sure" list based on new knowledge acquired during the training. As another variation, you might have learners cut and paste links to sites that represent what they "know for sure." This will add a web research component to the exercise and also reduce the amount of typing required.

What's My Line?

Overview	This icebreaker invites learners to attempt to guess the occupation of their classmates.
Objective	Introduce learners and explore career responsibilities.
Resources	None necessary
Delivery	Asynchronous discussion board forum
Process	Learners attempt to guess the occupation of classmates by reviewing clues and asking additional questions. Create a discussion board forum with the following instructions:

> *Add a thread to post three clues about your occupation in the discussion board forum. Your classmates will read the clues, may ask one additional "yes or no" question, and then try to guess your occupation by adding a thread to your post. You will need to check your thread frequently to both answer questions and identify correct guesses. This continues until someone guesses your occupation or we reach the deadline* (indicate last day to post guesses). *If we reach the deadline and no one guesses your occupation, please add a thread to post the correct answer.*
>
> *After you post your clues, review the clues posted by your fellow classmates and follow the directions described above to guess their occupations.*

Evaluation	Recognize those learners who make the most correct guesses and also those who were most active in their posts.
Variations	If classmates know each other well and are already familiar with each other's occupation, you might have them post their three clues anonymously so that the challenge is to not only to guess the occupation of the individuals but also their names.

You're the Expert

Overview	Learners share their particular area of expertise or knowledge with the class.
Objective	Learners gain recognition for their talents by sharing their areas of expertise along with practicing their internet research skills.
Resources	None necessary
Delivery	Asynchronous discussion board forum
Process	In a forum, provide the following directions:

We all have particular areas of expertise, something that we are good at or know a great deal about, from how to change a flat tire to how to play the cello. Tell us something that you can either do or know a great deal about; something that you could teach us. Note that it does not have to relate to the context of this course, but can be anything from belly dancing to trout fishing. We do not need all the details about the process, just provide the topical area, a bit about your experience or skill in this area, and a couple URLs to websites where we can learn more about this topic.

Note: You might start the first thread by providing your own "teachable" area and links.

Evaluation	No particular evaluation of areas of expertise is necessary, but you might provide recognition for those who find the most useful or interesting web resources.
Variations	Instead of identifying skills or expertise they currently possess, ask learners to identify something they would like to learn, not necessarily related to the course content, and then identify web resources relating to this topical area.

CHAPTER 5
Scenario Learning Activities

Scenario-based e-learning consists of highly engaging, authentic learning environments that allow trainees to solve authentic, work-based problems collaboratively anytime, anywhere. Scenario learning is the foundation of many learning techniques that involve role play, including case studies, problem-based learning, and goal-based scenarios. The idea behind scenario learning is that a good curriculum consists of a story in which learners play key roles. These roles are similar to those the trainee might actually perform in real life or might need to perform in the future. Trainees are placed within a realistic scenario where they take on the key role of the protagonist. They can work individually, but a team environment allows for a richer learning experience. Supporting materials and resources are provided, and trainers and online mentors are available to answer questions and provide guidance as needed. As trainees work through the scenario to achieve their mission, they learn the critical skills required to successfully accomplish their tasks. Because the scenario problems are based on authentic, work-based challenges, transfer to the work environment is seamless.

This section provides a series of role-based learning activities that involve authentic problems based on course content. You will create the actual case, problem, scenario, or role and tailor it to your course content. Writing a great scenario or case study is much like writing a one-act play. You need a hook to spark reader attention, well-developed characters, and realistic dialogue. All good stories have a few elements in common: They contain interesting characters who are involved in dramatic situations, and they have a point or a controlling idea. No one will be enthralled by a story that lacks these key elements. A truly dramatic moment has everything a good story needs—interesting characters in compelling situations who are wrestling with a big idea. Scenario writing is a three-stage process. Following is a brief explanation of each stage.

Stage One
- *Engage the learner:* What will cause the learner to become interested in reading this scenario?
- *Set up the conflict:* What is the main problem in the scenario?

Stage Two
- *Describe the struggle:* Why is this such a complex problem?
- *Create roadblocks:* What has happened in the organization, in the world, and/or between individuals to complicate the issue?
- *Present choices:* What are some possible solutions and the consequences of acting on those solutions?

Stage Three
- *Explain the defining action:* What happens in the organization or to individuals that "cause the light bulbs to go on"?
- *Force a choice:* How will you resolve the problem?

Consider adding authentic feedback to your scenario by having external experts review and comment on your learners' choices. Consider how solutions might affect the broader context in which they are set. To evaluate outcomes, you may also have learners work on real-life problems and send their solutions back to the organization that they would affect.

When designing your course, you may choose to adopt an overarching scenario, designed to run through the entire course lesson as in the example, "Diving into E-Learning," or you might use a short case, role play, or mini mystery at any point throughout the course to add excitement and realism. The use of a case may also establish an authentic context for the task at hand, so learners might see the application of acquired knowledge.

Goal-Based Scenarios

Overview	Learners take an active role in a realistic scenario that requires resolution.
Objective	Given a scenario, learners critically analyze the mission and produce a solution. In resolving the problem at hand, learners generate goals, are motivated to take action, and want to get involved in finding resolution.
Resources	Goals-based scenario, links to resources, and access to a mentor
Delivery	Include scenario in course content and support with e-mail access to a mentor, asynchronous discussion board forum, synchronous chat, and desktop collaboration software (see Addendum A for software recommendations).
Process	Goal-based scenarios differ from case studies in that the learner takes on the part of a character in the case. It requires not only narrative about the solution to the problem, but also the actual work production. Linked closely to a workplace problem, the product created to resolve the scenario can be used back on the job. Based on organizational training goals and performance gap analysis, create a goal-based scenario narrative (see characteristics of goal-based scenarios following this activity). Enhance your scenario with appropriate links to related sites, graphics (for example, photos of your characters), supporting documents, and so forth.

You may assign cases for individual analysis or team analysis. Team analysis might include follow-up discussion in a group-only forum, synchronous discussion in a live chat, and the use of desktop collaboration software to allow for the development of the team's solution document.

The resolution of the goal-based scenario requires the creation of a tangible product. In the sample scenario that follows, learners must create an e-learning strategy for their organization. You provide guidelines for the quality of the product to be designed, but there is no one correct resolution for a goal-based scenario; that is, in the example, there is no one correct format for developing an e-learning strategy. |
| *Evaluation* | Assess scenarios for the quality of the final product and also the depth of research that was conducted to arrive at the final resolution. |
| *Variations* | In addition to a resolution to the problem, have learners create a mindmap or flowchart that shows their process in resolving the conflict.

Ask learners to include a plan for using the scenario resolution back on the job. How might they implement their new strategy or product in the workplace? |

Writing Goal-Based Scenarios

1. *A good scenario has drama.* Embedded within the story should be a dramatic moment that reveals the character's conflict, as well as the main idea. If your scenario lacks drama, it will fail to garner the emotional response needed for the call to action. The goal-based scenario involves a compelling issue that arises at its beginning and sets the stage for a cascade of events to engage the learner.

2. *A good scenario reveals something new.* Your audience wants to find out something new about the character or the situation as your scenario progresses. Build suspense by adding new pieces of information about your characters and their dilemma as your story develops.

3. *A good scenario has a clear purpose.* If you find yourself wondering, "What's the point of this interaction?" then your purpose is not visible. The learner should come away with a clear idea of what must be done to resolve the problem.

4. *A good scenario is engaging.* You may have written a scene that moves the action forward, reveals something new, and has a clear purpose; but if you have not written it in a way that engages your audience, you have come up dry.

Sample Goal-Based Scenario Cover Story

Diving into E-Learning

It's Monday morning and you have just arrived at work when your telephone rings. It's the vice president of employee development, Karen Moore, and she asks if you have a few minutes to talk in her office. Of course you say yes. You gulp down the last of your Starbucks and off you go, wondering what's up. Is it good or bad news?

She greets you warmly, asking if you'd care for coffee or another beverage. Thinking of the vente latte you just downed, you decline. You sit on the edge of your chair, and Karen gets right to the point: "Our T & D effort is fragmented. We've got individual efforts going on throughout the company that aren't coordinated. We also do a poor job of tracking the learning efforts of our employees. On top of this, we've got to reduce our training delivery expenditures. Our CEO attended an executive leadership seminar and heard good things about e-learning. As you know, all our delivery currently takes place in the classroom, but he thinks we should consider converting most of it to online delivery. What do you think?"

Of course you've heard about this e-learning thing, but you really don't know enough to supply an educated opinion, so you take the politically correct, middle-of-the-road position: "It sounds very interesting," you say.

"I agree," says Karen. "It might just solve many of our problems. If nothing else, it will give us lots of visibility, which we need right now if we are to avoid layoffs." This e-learning solution is sounding better and better.

You're still wondering what all this has to do with you, but you're about to find out. "What we need is to identify a strategy for our e-learning initiative. We need a vision, a strategic plan that we can roll out and implement corporate wide. I think you are just the person to lead this effort." She sees the look of amazement on your face and assures, "Now I know you aren't an expert in this field, that you have a lot to learn, but it's so new that no one really knows much about it. I've chosen you to develop our strategic plan because you're smart, you have excellent communication skills, and you really understand our company. Who knows, maybe you can also use this as a project for one of the graduate classes you're taking at Roosevelt University. So what do you think?"

Feeling like you're about to jump off the high dive for the first time, you quickly decide, what the heck, this might be just the opportunity you need to move your career to the next level. "Thank you for this opportunity and for your faith in my ability," you reply. "Of course I'll lead the strategic effort. Exactly what deliverables are you looking for and when will you need them?"

"I'd like a comprehensive strategic plan for e-learning that addresses all the key issues: our vision for the future, how we'll go about designing our courses, the principles of adult learning that best apply to online delivery, and how we can make these courses interesting and engaging for our employees." You nod in agreement. This is stuff you know—it will just be a matter of applying it to virtual delivery. Karen continues, "I'd also like you to consider how we might incorporate knowledge management into our efforts." Here you're stumped. You've certainly heard of knowledge management but really don't have a good handle on it, but you nod again, not wanting to interrupt her momentum. "We also need to consider our culture. How can we help our employees and our trainers accept this change? Also, what skills will our employees need to become distance learners? What skills will our trainers need to develop to become online developers and facilitators? These are the questions I want you to address in your report. I see it being about five pages in length—our executive team doesn't have the attention span for any more than that. It might also contain some diagrams— you know, figures or graphs illustrating the points you make in your report. I'd like to have this on my desk by December 9th. Any questions?"

This is a lot to digest, so you say, "Not at this time, but I'm sure I'll need answers as I work through the process. Can I e-mail you?"

"Sure, anytime, but better yet, I have set up a worksite for you on Blackboard where you and your team can communicate, post questions and ideas, and I'll provide answers and directions. I think virtual communication is particularly appropriate here, don't you?"

You nod, thank Karen for her time, and head back to your office, feeling like you've taken the leap and are about to hit the water, wondering whether you will produce a swan dive or a belly flop. Of course, you've handled challenges like this before, so you feel confident that you can master the principles of e-learning and lead your company into the future.

Interactive Story

Overview	Learners collaborate to create an interactive story based on the course content. Learners take turns adding to the story in a discussion board forum until they reach an end.
Objective	Given a topic, learners add to the story content by creating a series of scenes or events.
Resources	None necessary
Delivery	Asynchronous discussion board forum
Process	Interactive stories have been around for some time and are one of the most popular text-based online games. Here you will create an interactive story with your class. Identify a topic and write an opening scene that lends itself to your content (see Example 1 following this activity). You may also want to add links to examples of interactive stories on the web. Provide the following instructions:

> *We are going to create an interactive story together that will allow us to further explore our course content. I'll get us started with the following opener* (provide opening event) *and you'll provide further developments. Jump in at any time and add to the story. Keep the title in mind and weave in our course content when you can. End each scene with a "cliffhanger" that leaves some aspect of the problem unresolved and lends itself to further action. Remember to add no more than two paragraphs of text at one time to stay within a reasonable length. You may come back as many as three times to add to the story.*

Note: You may either write a conclusion or ending to your story by a certain due date, or leave it open and create a never-ending story that learners can add to throughout the course.

Evaluation	Recognize learners for both the quantity and quality of their story lines, particularly those who use course content or principles in their scenes.
Variations	Rather than leaving the story completely open ended, you may want to add choices and then have your class write the scenes that might result from each choice (see Example 2 following this activity).

Example: Interactive Stories

Example 1: *Disappearing Benefits*

Possible related course topics or content: multiculturalism, employee benefits, corporate policy, conflict resolution.

Post the following opening scene as a discussion board forum:

> "I can't believe this. They've eliminated flex time, done away with job sharing, are closing the on-site day care center, and are even threatening to reduce that wonderful family leave policy that gave us an extra two weeks off for emergencies," said Marcie, a working mother of three who has been with the company for ten years.
>
> "We fought hard for these changes," said Jennie, her co-worker. "Why are they doing this to us?"
>
> "Something about budget cuts and all extra benefits have to go. Well, this isn't an extra benefit for me, but allows me to work and take care of my family at the same time. I can't sit still for this. I'm going to fight this," resolved Marcie.

Note: Here learners continue the story by adding additional scenes. Ideally, each scene should end as a cliffhanger which encourages continued action.

Example 2: *Disappearing Benefits (Add Choices)*

Using the previous scenario, add the following choices as threads to your forum.

A. Marcie goes directly to the union to file a grievance.
B. Marcie goes to her supervisor and asks for support.
C. Marcie starts a petition and gets signatures from fifty of her co-workers.

Instruct learners to select a choice and write the scene that might follow if the main character were to choose that course of action. You can continue to add additional choices to each course of action, weaving an intricate story.

Mini MOO

Overview	Create a synchronous chat that has the characteristics of a MOO, or virtual reality environment, where learners take on roles to discuss course-related issues.
Objective	Learners formulate a character and role, and engage in synchronous discussion of course-related issues.
Resources	Location for the interaction and a selection of possible roles or characters
Delivery	Synchronous chat in small groups
Process	A MOO (multiuser domain object oriented) is a computer program that allows multiple users to connect via the internet to a shared database of rooms and other objects and interact with each other and the database in synchronous time. In the MOO, you can do many of the things possible in real life: talk to others, look around, explore the environment, and interact with things you find along the way. It is a great way to facilitate real-time learning and discussion. Unfortunately, MOOs are rather complicated to design and use, requiring special software and a server. In this exercise, you can give your learners a taste of "mooing" in a simple chat room.

One of the cornerstones of the MOO experience involves taking on a character or role in the interaction. Begin by placing learners into groups of four to five individuals. Thus, you will need to recreate the MOO experience for each group in your class.

Create a "room" or location for their interaction (the board room, employee cafeteria, coffee shop, etc.) and provide a visual description of the location. Next provide a list of possible characters (names, gender, and job titles) and allow trainees to choose their characters. Once each person has chosen a character, they add a thread to the discussion board forum to provide a detailed character description (physical appearance, age, personality). Learners may print out a hard copy of the character descriptions for use in the live chat.

Begin the "mini MOO" by asking group members to log on to the chat room. At least for the first session, you will need to be present to facilitate the discussion. Feel free to take on a role yourself and interact "in role" with the group members. Set the stage by adding the description of your room and then have each group introduce themselves using their character's name and adding their prepared description. To begin the conversation, provide a topic for discussion that relates to your course content. Invite learners to respond in role as their characters would. Allow the conversation to continue for a set time and schedule another chat session to continue the current discussion or address a new topic.

Evaluation	Recognize learners for participating in lively discussion and for having the flexibility in their thinking to take on a character or role that is different.
Variations	Encourage learners to take on roles that are different from their own in job function, gender, or age, to allow them to experience a new perspective.
	If time and resources permit, explore the creation of an actual MOO environment (see Addendum A for software and online resources).

The Mini Mystery

Overview	Everyone loves a mystery. Here learners solve a brief, interactive mystery based on course content.
Objective	Given a set of clues, solve a content-related "crime," and deduce the most likely outcome. Involve the application of critical thinking and synthesis to consider a series of events and predict outcomes.
Resources	Develop a brief mystery plot based on your course content containing a protagonist (main character), potential villains, and clues.
Delivery	Asynchronous, text-based delivery that can be an individual or group project, discussion board post, or quiz question; asynchronous video or audio delivery; synchronous delivery via a live chat or MOO
Process	Using principles included in your course content, develop a short mystery story, two to three paragraphs in length. For example, you might use the title, "The Mystery of the Lost Customer" in a service training program, or "The Mystery of the Tardy Employee" in a management skills course. Include a main character, a dramatic event that must be explained or solved, clues, and an open ending that asks learners for resolution (see the example following this activity). Learners might "solve" the mystery by identifying the "culprit" (can be a guilty person or process) and recommend actions that might be taken to prevent future crimes or negative events. Depending on your delivery method, learners can e-mail their guesses or post them in the discussion board.
Evaluation	Recognize learners for both their effort in attempting to solve the mystery and their correct solutions.
Variations	Rather than including all clues in the initial presentation, provide one new clue each day so learners attempt to solve the mystery with the least number of possible clues.

Example: The Mini Mystery

Setting: an online course in service management, restaurant operations, or quality management

The Mystery of the Lost Customer

Robert Jones owns a fine-dining restaurant with a discriminating clientele. One of his most frequent customers, Mr. London, had been dining with him for several years, averaging two visits per month. In March, Robert noticed that he hadn't seen Mr. London for some time. Checking past records, he discovered that London's last visit had been in mid December, prior to the holidays. Robert decided to give Mr. London a call to see if there had been any difficulties. Mr. London revealed little information, saying that "quality just wasn't up to par" and that he wouldn't be back. He refused to provide further details or to come back, even with the offer of complimentary meals.

Robert kept a detailed history and examined the records from the night of Mr. London's last visit. The records indicated that he had tried a new menu item featuring salmon. It also looked as though his server had been Steve, a long-time employee. Robert remembered that he had been off that night, celebrating his wife's birthday, so he had no firsthand knowledge of the evening's events. Why did Mr. London refuse to return? What aspect of his experience wasn't up to par?

Notes: Clues are purposely limited and vague. You may provide further clues or information in response to learners' questions, or add a clue each day to the discussion board or in the announcements section until the mystery is solved. Have a correct answer in mind, such as, "Mr. London had been put off that night because his waiter, Steve, smelled of alcohol and cigarettes, his hair looked dirty, and there were grease spots on his white apron. Mr. London is very fastidious and couldn't even finish his meal due to his server's unclean appearance. London was also embarrassed because he had brought in dinner guests. He vowed never to return." You may either provide the correct answer as soon as the mystery is solved, or wait and give everyone a chance to take a guess and then provide the answer.

Problem-Based E-Learning

Overview	Learners work with online references to solve an ill-structured, course-related problem.
Objective	Given a problem situation, learners will work collaboratively to analyze the problem, collect research information, and formulate a solution.
Resources	Access to knowledge base or research links
Delivery	Asynchronous delivery
Process	Trainees are presented with a work-based, ill-structured (limited detail and no clear solution) problem to solve collaboratively. Guidelines for implementing problem-based learning follow this exercise. First, select a problem and deliver it to learners via the assignment section or discussion board. Next create a series of five forums in each group discussion board where learners can post their progress.

Forum 1 Learners describe the problem and ask learners to detail their current knowledge of the situation.

Forum 2 Learners refine their problem statement.

Forum 3 Learners determine what they need to know to solve the problem.

Forum 4 Research results are posted.

Forum 5 Contains the resolution to the problem. The final summary statement of the resolution is also posted to the general discussion board so it may be shared with the entire class.

Then, place learners in groups and assign the following responsibilities:

1. Summarize current knowledge.
2. Create a problem statement.
3. Identify "what we need to know."
4. Create a problem resolution statement.

Next provide the following instructions in the assignment section of your course:

In this assignment you will have the opportunity to work together in solving a problem similar to those you experience at work. In groups, you will identify, collect, integrate, synthesize, and apply learning resources related to the problem, to find a resolution. Here is the process you will follow in investigating and resolving the problem.

1. In the group discussion board, add a thread to respond to the posted question in Forum 1 to indicate what you already know about the problem. This might include data from the problem situation along with your prior knowledge and experience. One group member should then catalogue your collective knowledge by creating a summary statement. Post this at the end of the forum.

2. *Another learner will create a problem statement and post it as a thread to the second question on your group board in Forum 2. A problem statement should come from your group's analysis of what you know. The problem statement will probably need refining as new information is discovered and brought to bear on the situation. Typical problem statements may be based on discrepant events, incongruities, anomalies, or stated needs of a client. After the statement is posted, other group members should review it and add additional suggestions as necessary until a final consensus is reached as to the nature of the problem at hand.*

3. *A third learner will add a thread to answer the next question in Forum 3 in your group board: "What do we need to know?" Others should add their ideas and thoughts as to what information must be gathered to solve the problem. Each learner will work independently to gather information and bring it back to the group.*

4. *In the fourth forum, each member will post the results of their research including links to appropriate websites and articles.*

Once all the research information is posted, each learner should add a thread to the fifth forum to answer the question, "What should we do?" When all the answers are in, one learner will summarize the ideas in a resolution statement. The resolution statement is then posted to the general discussion board for review by the entire class.

Evaluation

There is no correct answer in problem-based learning, but the focus of evaluation is on the research and collective wisdom that results. Recognize group efforts where a wide range of ideas and resources are generated. Also look for depth in problem resolution. Ideally, resolutions will address the concerns of various stakeholders and anticipate and plan for additional difficulties and conflict.

Variations

Vary your level of involvement and guidance depending on the experience of your learners. Answer the question "What do we need to know" for the learners by suggesting topics to explore. Rather than leaving the research process open ended, provide specific links to sites and sources where information may be collected.

Good Problems

A critical factor in the success of problem-based learning is the problem itself. Effective problems have the following characteristics.[34]

1. The real-world authenticity engages the learner's interest and ensures they have a stake in solving the problem.
2. The motivational dimension encourages learners to persevere in probing for a deeper understanding of concepts.
3. The inbuilt expectation is that the learners will make judgments and decisions based on facts, the information they acquire, and their application of rational thinking; and that they will defend their decisions in line with the principles being learned.
4. Cooperation between learners is an essential element of the problem-solving process, with this element recognized by the learners.
5. The initial questions provided in the problem should draw all learners into discussion and encourage them to continue to draw on each others' knowledge. These questions should be open-ended, thus inviting a range of responses; connected to previous knowledge, thus valuing all contributions; and focused on unresolved or controversial issues, thus eliciting diverse opinions.
6. Learners must engage in higher order thinking.

Example: "Strike Three, You're Out"

The following problem might be used in a training program that addresses hotel management or human resource issues.

Tomorrow, 500 convention guests will arrive at 9:00 A.M. and plan to check into the Goldstone, a large downtown convention hotel, to begin their week of meetings, luncheons, and dinners. Mr. Regis, the general manager, has just learned that the local hotel and restaurant worker's union has called a strike and all member employees will support it. In just one hour, all servers, cooks, dishwashers, bell attendants, and housekeepers will leave the premises. It is too late to cancel the convention as many of the guests are already in transit. Other hotels in the city are also affected by the strike, so walking guests is not an option.

Role Play

Overview	Learners participate in a role play delivered synchronously through online chat.
Objective	Internalize course principles and apply them in a role play situation.
Resources	Role play descriptions
Delivery	Synchronous chat
Process	A synchronous chat open to the entire class or to a group provides an excellent medium for traditional role play. Learners might practice interview skills, sales calls, problem solving, coaching, or any number of course-related skills through online, real-time communication. Set up the problem situation, provide specific roles, and instruct learners to log in to a chat room in groups with the remainder of the class observing. If learners are new to role play and chat, provide specific questions for their discussion. If you have seasoned role players, provide a loosely devised situation and let the trainees respond. You as the trainer might also take on one of the roles to model the desired behavior, to elicit response from the trainees. In this case, have the class log on to the chat so they might observe your interaction with the trainee. Please note that virtual role play requires active imagination and may be difficult for some learners to conceive your purpose. Additional support may be required in the form of a practice session. Although online role play does not allow for nonverbal cues, the entire role play script can be saved for analysis.
Evaluation	After the role play is conducted, send learners a checklist via e-mail so that trainees can examine the script and identify specific skills.
Variations	Ask learners to review the saved role play script and "rewrite" their lines. Given time for review and consideration, how would they change their response?

Seven-Jump Method

Overview	Use the seven-jump method[35] to analyze and solve an online case or problem.
Objective	Given a problem or case situation, learners analyze the issues, propose tentative solutions, research additional information, and evaluate solutions.
Resources	Case or problem situation
Delivery	Asynchronous discussion board forum
Process	Working in teams, learners will practice the seven-jump method to analyze, brainstorm, and evaluate possible solutions.

Present learners with a case or problem delivered in the course assignment section or in a discussion board post. Next, assign learners to study groups and provide the following instructions:

> *You will be using the following Seven-Jump Method to solve a course-related problem. Meet with your team members (specify meeting methods: chat, instant messaging, virtual work space, group discussion board) and complete and document each step of the process.*
>
> *Post your notes from each step in the group discussion board forum for this assignment.*

Seven Jump Method
1. *Identify and define unknown terms and concepts.*
2. *Identify and describe the problem in the case.*
3. *Analyze the problem by brainstorming possible solutions.*
4. *Critique the results of your brainstorming session and choose the most appropriate solutions.*
5. *Define the learning issues and objectives. What must you learn to implement the solutions?*
6. *Engage in self-directed study to collect information and knowledge to fill the gaps specified by the learning issues.*
7. *Synthesize the information and evaluate its utility in resolving the original problem.*

Evaluation	Ask one group member to post his or her completed assignment in a general discussion board so that all group work is shared with the entire class. Recognize groups for the depth of their research and the feasibility of their solutions.
Variations	Create groups of seven people and assign each group member a step in the process to lead. That member initiates his or her step and guides the group through discussion and research related to that particular step in the process.

Virtual Case Study

Overview	In groups or individually, learners solve complex problems delivered in a case study format.
Objective	Given a case situation, learners analyze the problem and formulate a detailed solution.
Resources	Online case study
Delivery	Include case in course site and support with asynchronous discussion board forum, synchronous chat, and desktop collaboration software (see Addendum A for software recommendations).
Process	Case studies provide a familiar and well-structured system for incorporating either individual or group problem solving. The first step is to develop a case study, either real or fictitious (see guidelines for case development following this activity). Enhance your virtual case with appropriate links to related sites, graphics (for example, photos of your fictitious characters), supporting documents, and so forth.
	You may assign cases for individual analysis or team analysis. Team analysis might include follow-up discussion in a group-only forum, synchronous discussion in a live chat, and the use of desktop collaboration software to allow for the development of the team's solution document. The case solution might be presented in several ways. It could include a post to a discussion board forum so that each individual and/or group can review the solutions of others. You might require a visual presentation of the case solution in the form of a PowerPoint presentation, or you might have a supplemental quiz that tests knowledge and understanding of the case resolution.
Evaluation	Cases typically have a "correct answer," so recognize those learners or groups that identify the correct choice or strategy. You might also recognize the critical thinking skills of those teams that may not choose the correct path, but identify alternative strategies that have potential merit.
Variations	Most cases are fictitious, but you might include real people and real dilemmas in your study. This adds a sense of reality to the project, particularly if your learners can have access to the people in the case as either a guest speaker or via e-mail to ask questions and to delve more deeply into the problem.
	You might also incorporate mini case studies throughout your course to quickly gauge understanding and create immediacy.

Example: Writing the Virtual Case Study: 101

Creating a virtual case is much like developing a traditional text-based case study with a few twists. As in traditional case design, begin by developing your content, using the following suggestions.

◆ Base content on key problems faced in the workplace.
◆ Make sure that the skills your audience practices as they solve your case correspond to your course objectives.
◆ Decide whether you will use a real or fictitious problem.
◆ Collect or create supporting documents.
◆ Identify useful web-based resources (portals, links, white papers, etc.).
◆ Identify your main characters.
◆ Create interesting content.
◆ Use third-person narrative.
◆ Add dialogue when possible.
◆ Use sufficient detail to portray the problem at hand, but also create the need for additional use of resources and outside research.
◆ Include a series of questions for learners to answer that guide the resolution of the case.
◆ Ask learners to not only describe their resolution of the case problem, but also to detail the process they used to arrive at this resolution.
◆ Add "virtual excitement" to your case by including photographs, actual supporting documents, links to additional sites, and opportunities for synchronous online discussion between team members.

Who Am I?

Overview	Learners take on the persona of a famous person or theorist while classmates attempt to guess their identity.
Objective	Research a particular leader or theorist and internalize his or her principles.
Resources	None necessary
Delivery	Asynchronous discussion board forum or synchronous delivery through a live chat or MOO
Process	First, send each learner an e-mail to assign a "secret" theorist or leader that pertains to your course content. Then create a forum in the discussion board that instructs learners to post clues about their identity. Provide the following directions in your e-mail:

This is a simple role play exercise where each of you will take on the role of a prominent leader that pertains to our course (management theorists, marketing geniuses, CEOs, etc.). *Your assigned leader is* (assign each class member or group member a different leader). *Be sure to keep your assignment secret from your classmates as they will be attempting to guess your identity in the next part of the exercise.*

Go to the discussion board forum where I have posted the following question for you to answer (this should be a general, open-ended question relating to your course content, such as, "How might we motivate our employees?" or "How might we increase sales?"). *Please respond to the question "in role" or as your assigned leader might respond. To do this well, you must research the ideals and principles held by your leader so you can provide realistic and specific answers containing subtle hints of your identity.*

Come back to the boards later in the week, when everyone has had a chance to respond, and add a thread to each class member's response to attempt to guess the identities.

Evaluation	Recognize learners for both the accuracy of their guesses and the quality of their posts. Those who created detailed answers to your content-related questions that contained accurate but subtle clues should be applauded.
	You might also use the content of the learner responses to create matching quiz questions, where the class attempts to match the correct leader to the appropriate ideals or principles.
Variations	Instead of taking on the roles of people, learners might role-play the components of a process, a market segment, or a type of customer.

CHAPTER 6
Peer Learning

Peer support is an invaluable resource in a training or educational environment. Belonging to a network, or community of learners, can facilitate successful completion of educational and training programs. Peer support is vital in a virtual environment that can leave learners feeling disconnected from the instructor, the other learners, and the course itself.[36] Connections with fellow learners can create a sense of camaraderie that can overcome the feelings of loneliness and disconnection that lead to high rates of dropout in virtual learning.

In traditional training, peer support often develops independently of the course itself. Learners get together on break or after class to discuss course content, clarify issues, or even commiserate. In e-learning environments, communities of support do not materialize independently; opportunities for connection must be embedded in the course design. It is your job to bring people together in your courses in ways that support the development of shared meaning, mentoring relationships, and peer-to-peer learning. You must incorporate opportunities for learners to work together to share ideas, problems, and knowledge. Peer-to-peer learning involves more than simply working through team projects or participating in group discussion. It is the development and maintenance of supportive relationships among learners. In this section, you will find a series of activities that promote peer-to-peer learning from mentoring and study buddies to the sharing of course-related problems and work-based challenges. An excellent time to incorporate such exercises is early in the course, shortly after an icebreaker or session opener. At this time, learners are getting to know each other, starting to feel confident, and are ready to develop relationships and share ideas and knowledge. Peer-to-peer learning opportunities can continue the positive momentum created by your opening exercises.

Buddy System

Overview	Working in pairs, learners communicate with their partner regularly to complete assignments, discuss coursework, and provide feedback.
Objective	Provide learners with a greater sense of connection by placing them in pairs so they can facilitate and support each other's online learning experience.
Resources	Instant messaging host
Delivery	Asynchronous delivery via discussion board post and synchronous delivery through chat and instant messaging
Process	At the beginning of the course, pair each learner with another classmate. Provide short, weekly assignments that keep learners in continuous contact with each other via e-mail, instant messaging, and private chat or via the telephone. These brief assignments might be course related and involve the following:

1. Interview your partner to find out his or her reaction to the week's lesson.
2. Develop review questions to prepare for a quiz.
3. Compare assignments.
4. Complete joint assignments.

Evaluation	Ask learners to send you an activity report, describing the ways they are interacting and working with their partners. Recognize the pairs who are most supportive and connected.
Variations	From time to time, intersperse the content-related assignments with some less serious assignments:

Send your learning buddy an online greeting card, discuss favorite movies, sports, recipes, websites, or share a favorite joke (clean, politically correct).

Dear Abby

Overview	A discussion board forum in the form of an advice column provides solutions to content-based problems.
Objective	Learners report content-based problems that need resolution and evaluate the appropriateness of solutions provided by others.
Resources	None necessary
Delivery	Asynchronous discussion board forum
Process	Create a sort of online "Dear Abby" forum where participants can post problems for resolution. Title the forum "Dear Abby" (or substitute the name of your favorite advice columnist) and provide the following instructions:

> *Everyone is familiar with advice columns, in which people write letters describing problems and the columnist provides a solution. In addition, the original person with the problem or other readers come back and tell Dear Abby that she missed the boat on this one, and provide additional solutions. Writers can either include their real names or an anonymous name.*
>
> *Our advice column will work much like this: Here, I'd like you to bring real problems that you or your co-workers face on the job that relate to (your course topic). I will play Dear Abby and attempt to give you a viable solution to your problem. Feel free to contest my solutions if you think they won't work. Do this by adding a thread to my original solution. You may also "write in" to comment on the solutions I provide others, by adding a thread to that post and indicating why you think it won't work and providing an alternative solution. You may make your posts anonymously, meaning that your classmates won't know who you are, but I will still be able to see your identity.*

Evaluation	Recognize learners for their active participation in the forum and for the quality of the solutions they offer.
Variations	Instead of taking the role of "Dear Abby" yourself, assign it to a learner. This assignment might rotate throughout the semester (each learner is Dear Abby for a few days). This person is responsible for checking the board and providing solutions to all problems posted during his or her role time period.

Personal Ads

Overview	Learners create personal ads based on a need or issue within their organization.
Objective	Identify an area of need within the organization and construct a personal ad that requests a response.
Resources	None
Delivery	Asynchronous discussion board forum
Process	Create a forum in the discussion board that contains the following assignment:

> *Perhaps one of the most amazing developments in our culture is the personal ad. In this assignment, you will create a "personal ad" not to attract dates of course, but to attract ideas and solutions to significant problems you face in your organization. For example, if your organization was finding it difficult to provide quality training experiences at a reasonable cost, your ad might read:*
>
> *"Wanted, high-quality, cost-effective training for a small retail business. Enjoy lots of active learning, detailed course objectives, authentic practice, and evaluation. Must show return on investment. If you enjoy working with enthusiastic learners in a creative, dynamic setting, please reply."*
>
> *Your ads can address issues relating to procedures, policies, marketing, human resources, etc. Quality ads that generate lots of response will contain details about the characteristics of your organization and your need. Please add a thread to this forum to post your ad, then come back later in the week and read and reply to the messages posted by your fellow classmates. Your responses to their ads should include ideas or links to sites that might help them find a solution to their problem.*

Evaluation	Look for ads that are creative, detailed, and generate response. In addition, recognize learners for both the quantity and quality of the response they provide to the ads of others.
Variations	Create a "personal ad quiz" where you write mini ads looking for particular theories or principles you have covered in your class. Learners respond to the ads by identifying the theory or concept that you are seeking.

Push It to Me

Overview	Using the principle of "push technology," learners send each other up-to-date information regarding course content.
Objective	Using internet search tools, learners identify the latest developments and send links to appropriate sites to their classmates via e-mail.
Resources	E-mail address list for class
Delivery	Asynchronous delivery via e-mail
Process	In push technology, prespecified information is automatically sent to individuals usually by way of e-mail. Here learners will reap the benefits of push technology by keeping each other abreast of the latest course-related trends.

First, compose a list of e-mail addresses for your class. Make sure that these are addresses learners do not mind sharing with their classmates. Then post the following assignment:

> *Push technology allows web users to receive up-to-the-minute information about specific fields or topics. In this assignment, you will create our own "push" by taking turns researching new developments* (related to course topic) *and sending bulletins to your classmates. Each* (day or week depending on course duration), *a different classmate will act as "scanner" to sift through the information on the web relating to* (course topic) *and send or push an e-mail bulletin to the entire class detailing the findings. Two or three URLs should be included for more detail. Please see the attached assignment list to find out when you will be the scanner. Send your e-mail to the entire class, including the instructor, on the exact date assigned.*

Evaluation	Recognize learners for the value and timeliness of information they "push" to their fellow classmates.
Variations	Rather than sending e-mail messages, updates could be posted asynchronously in a "push" board. Create a forum and have learners add information on their assigned date, ensuring that new information is generated throughout the course period.

Scripted Cooperation

Overview	In pairs, learners practice scripted cooperation,[37] where they review and facilitate understanding and transfer of course content.
Objective	Given course content, learners will summarize and communicate their understanding of the material to their partner and then predict the transfer of the knowledge to their workplace.
Resources	None necessary
Delivery	Synchronous chat, instant message, or e-mail
Process	Arrange the class into learning pairs. Post the following instructions in the assignment section of course:

Working in pairs, you will share your understanding of the course material with your partner. First read (assigned passage) and then meet with your partner (synchronous meeting via chat, instant messaging, or asynchronous meeting via e-mail). Complete the following process:

1. *Learner 1 summarizes the first half (or segment) of the content for learner 2.*
2. *Learner 2 adds to the summary.*
3. *Both identify ways they would use the information to solve a workplace problem.*
4. *Next reverse roles and complete the same process for the second half of the reading assignment.*
5. *Keep a written transcript of your process and post it to the discussion board (or e-mail to instructor).*

Evaluation	Recognize transfer plans or ways learners will use the course information to solve a workplace problem.
Variations	Learning pairs can also quiz each other in preparation for an exam, review and provide feedback on course assignments, answer questions, and, in general, support each other throughout the course.

Secret Mentor

Overview	Learners mentor each other anonymously via e-mail.
Objective	Learners form valuable helping relationships while also identifying and communicating important course resources.
Resources	Links to sites that offer anonymous e-mail
Delivery	Asynchronous delivery via e-mail
Process	At the start of the course, assign each learner to act as the "secret mentor" of a classmate. Throughout the course, using anonymous e-mail, the mentor sends the mentee encouraging messages, useful links to helpful course information, ideas or suggestions, and so forth, without revealing his or her identity. At the end of the semester, ask learners to try to guess the identity of their mentors.
Evaluation	You might ask mentees to evaluate the mentoring skills of their partners by sending you an e-mail describing the quantity and quality of their mentor's help. As a second follow-up, when their mentor's identity is revealed, mentees might send a thank-you note to their mentor.
Variations	You might assign mentors publicly, revealing the identity of their mentors upfront and eliminating the need for anonymous e-mail. Let the students know that they will be receiving unsolicited help and information from their mentors during the class and that their mentor is someone who they can go to for help and advice.

Story Board

Overview	Shared meaning is created when learners post and respond to stories about personal experiences with course-related issues.
Objective	Learners construct narratives of events that relate to the course content so that others might benefit from their experiences.
Resources	None necessary
Delivery	Asynchronous discussion board forum
Process	Create a discussion board forum where learners share stories.[38] Give the board a focus or title (most embarrassing moment, worst job interview, worst customer service experience) that is based on the course content. Provide the following directions:

We all enjoy a good story and learn a great deal from the experiences of others. Share your stories about (course-related topic) by posting them on the discussion board. Read the stories of others and add a thread to their story to let them know if you have had similar experiences or find their narrative useful.

Evaluation	Recognize learners for their openness in sharing their experiences and also for the detail they provide in their stories.
Variations	Rather than content-based stories, this exercise can serve as an icebreaker by having learners post personal experiences (best day of my life, most inspiring moment, best vacation, etc.).

CHAPTER 7
Content Review and Practice

Active e-learning involves and engages trainees in the acquisition of new skills and knowledge. In active learning, students are fully engrossed and engaged in doing things and thinking about what they are doing.[39] Learners engage in higher order thinking tasks such as analysis, synthesis, and evaluation. Active learning promotes increased ability to utilize the cognitive skills of objectivity, creative thinking, judgment, interpretation, and problem solving while enhancing their affective behaviors.[40]

As in a traditional setting, e-learners prefer strategies that promote active learning over traditional lectures and testing. They would rather "do something" with the course material than simply memorize it. But how do you transform the principles of active learning to web-based learning?

This section contains a variety of active learning exercises that are fun, interesting, and engaging. They involve the learner in the course content in ways that memorization and test-taking could never accomplish. You will find a series of exercises that challenge the learner to engage in authentic practice, seek out answers, and gain feedback and recognition for their performance.

Backward Quiz

Overview	Rather than asking learners to provide answers, create a discussion board quiz where learners provide the questions.
Objective	Given an answer to a quiz question, learners use course content to develop the corresponding question.
Resources	None necessary
Delivery	Asynchronous discussion board forum
Process	Students are accustomed to quizzes and reviews that ask for the correct answer, but this exercise will reverse the process. Identify a series of terms or objective facts relating to your course and post these in a discussion board forum:

> *Now that you have thoroughly reviewed our course content, it's time for a quiz. But instead of asking you for answers, I'm asking you for questions. Using my answers, identify questions that you might ask to arrive at these answers. Next, go to the forum in the discussion board and post each question that you have identified, but keep the answers to yourself for now. The second part of this assignment involves answering questions posted by your classmates. Check the boards frequently and if you know the correct answer to a question posted by a classmate, add a thread and post your answer. Keep coming back and try to answer as many questions correctly as you can. The first person who answers each question correctly wins the point.*

Evaluation	Tally the number of correct answers for each class member and recognize the winner. Also recognize those learners who crafted questions that were both detailed and easy to comprehend.
Variations	Use the content of the forum to create a follow-up quiz or test.

Chain Letter

Overview	Learners participate in creating a chain letter by writing and answering content-related review questions.
Objective	Using course content, respond to an open-ended review question and then, also using content, formulate a new review question.
Resources	E-mail distribution list
Delivery	E-mail and asynchronous discussion board forum
Process	Send the following instructions to all learners via e-mail:

> *We are going to create a chain letter to review the material we have covered so far in the course.* (Be sure to note the course content they may use as their source, such as page numbers or URL.) *No, you don't have to send any money, and nothing terrible will happen to you or your family if you don't participate! This is a good chain letter. I'll start us off with a question and send it to the first person on the distribution list.* (Attach a distribution list containing e-mail addresses or post it in your course site and remind learners of its location.) *This person will then answer the question using the course content and write a new question, forwarding it to the second person. The second person will answer the question, write a new one, and forward it to the third person on the list and so on, until everyone has participated. The last person on the list will forward the rather large e-mail to me and I will post the content in our discussion board so you can all see the results.*

Note: Also include a statement about turnaround time. Ideally, learners will answer their question and create a new one within 24 hours of receiving the e-mail. If for some reason they cannot meet the deadline, ask them to simply forward the e-mail to the next person on the list. If time allows, you may have the nonparticipants reenter the game at the end.

Start the game with the first question, sending it to the first person on your list. When you receive the final list of all questions and answers, post them in the discussion board so all can see the work that was created.

Evaluation	Review the content of the answers developed by the learners for accuracy and thoroughness. Also consider the quality of the review questions written by each learner. How detailed were the questions? Did they provide enough direction and information to generate rich answers?
Variations	To make further use of the information generated by learners, use the questions and answers to create a quiz, test, or game as a follow-up.

Content Scavenger Hunt

Overview	This content-based scavenger hunt asks learners to search for terms as they review course materials.
Objective	Increase motivation and cognitive process as learners review course content material by having them search for specific pieces of information.
Resources	Scavenger hunt questions
Delivery	Asynchronous delivery
Process	Create a series of questions that can be answered by learners either individually or in teams as they review course content materials (either electronic or text based). In a team environment, learners post their answers in a group discussion board so that all team members may share them. Follow up with an online quiz based on the questions and their answers.
Evaluation	Recognize both the team who locates the most correct answers and the individual who achieves the highest quiz score.
Variations	Rather than a scavenger hunt based on course content, develop questions that can be answered by searching the web. Learners then post both the answer and link to the site where they found the information.

Cut and Paste

Overview	This virtual communication exercise allows learners the chance to see that the message can be changed by simply rearranging the sentence order.[41]
Objective	Given an e-mail where sentences have been jumbled, learners rearrange them and then determine the message that is being conveyed.
Resources	A jumbled e-mail that deals with course content
Delivery	E-mail or asynchronous discussion board forum
Process	Here the sentences of a simple letter have been jumbled and learners re-arrange the letter as they think it was meant to be read. Place the jumbled letter in the assignments section of the course, post it in a forum, or send it directly to learners via e-mail with the following instructions:

Here is an e-mail message that has been jumbled so that the sentences are not in the correct order. Using your word processor and the cut and paste commands, rearrange the jumbled sentences to create a letter that makes sense to you.

Note: Have learners either e-mail the letter to you and then you post all letters to the board later so you can keep each person's results hidden until all respond, or have each person post his or her letter to the board. The letters will have surprisingly different meanings depending on the order of the sentences.

Evaluation	Follow up with an additional forum where learners discuss the variations in meaning that can result from something so simple as sentence order.
Variations	Rather than giving learners jumbled sentences, give them a topic or message that their e-mail should address and have each learner compose their own message. Post the messages and examine the variety of ways that learners have communicated the same message.

Do You See What I Think?

Overview	This exercise combines procedural writing and visual learning. One class member creates a written description of a process, then his or her partner uses this description to create a visual diagram. The two are compared to see how closely they match.
Objective	Using a course content-based process, learners work in pairs to first develop a written description of the process and then construct a visual depiction.
Resources	Visual diagramming software (mindmap, concept map, graph, etc.) (see Addendum A for software recommendations).
Delivery	Asynchronous delivery; learners utilize e-mail and follow-up questions are posted in the discussion board.
Process	Assign learners a partner by posting a list of paired class members in the body of the assignment description, via e-mail or in the announcement section of the course. Then provide the following instructions:

> *When we hear or read information, we often create visual images or pictures of the content in our minds. In this exercise, we will learn more about the accuracy of these visual images as we review our course content. You have each been assigned a partner. The first member of each pair will create a detailed written description of a process that relates to the course content. (You may either assign the same process to all pairs or different processes to each pair.) E-mail this written description to your partner.*
>
> *The second team member, working with the written description only, creates a process map that visually depicts the written description. This visual might be in the form of a mindmap, concept map, chart, or diagram (see Addendum A for recommended software).*
>
> *The second partner will post both the written description and mindmap to the discussion board section so other class members can review them.* (Note that in most instances, everyone must have the software loaded on their computers to open the graphic documents.)

Follow up with discussion questions that ask the pairs to describe their challenges in completing the project. Was it difficult to visualize another person's thoughts? Did the visual depiction match the written description? What changes would you make to both the written description and visual now that you see them together?

Evaluation	Consider how closely the visual depiction represents the written description of the process. How well did the first person describe the process? How accurate was the visual depiction of this process?
Variations	To add more challenge, ask the first person to create a written description of a process, but without revealing the actual name of the process. The partner then creates a visual depiction of the process while attempting to identify the name of the process.

Every Picture Tells a Story

Overview	Learners examine a series of photos depicting people, situations, or interactions and interpret what they see.
Objective	Given a series of photos depicting people in work-based situations, learners will interpret the interaction and draw conclusions regarding what they see.
Resources	Obtain photographs of people involved in activities or interacting in situations that reflect the course content (job interview, coaching, sales, customer service, team planning, etc.) saved as image files, PowerPoint presentation, or digital photo album (see software recommendations in Addendum A). Photos may be royalty free from the web or your own digital shots.
Delivery	Asynchronous in assignment section followed by discussion board forum
Process	In this exercise, learners will attach meaning to images and discuss the similarities and differences in their interpretations. Locate or create a series of pictures of people. Depending on your course, these might depict people diverse in age, gender, or race, or pictures that depict scenes or actions relating to your course content (conflict situation with co-worker or customer, sales meeting, work group meeting). Post these photos to your site in the assignments section, making sure that each photo is numbered (attach photos as files, create short PowerPoint show, or use digital photo album). Also create a discussion board forum for assignment posting and provide the following instructions:

> *Examine the photographs and tell us what you think is happening in each. What types of people are in the photos? What might you guess about them? What is happening in the scene? What might be the outcome? Summarize your response to each photo (be sure to number each comment so it corresponds to the representative photo). Review the posts of others to see if they drew the same conclusions as you.*

Follow up with a summary post where you discuss the various ways that situations might be interpreted and the results of "drawing conclusions" based only on visual input.

Evaluation	Look for a variety of interpretations of the action in the photographs. Recognize learners for the detail they provide in their conclusions.
Variations	Learners can create their own storyboards of work-based situations using freeware or trial downloads of storyboard software (see Addendum A for software suggestions).

Hotlist

Overview	Learners create a hotlist or annotated bibliography of their course topic in an exercise that both provides practice in web research and creates a reserve of resources for your class.
Objective	Use internet search engines to locate course-related sources and chronicle these in a hotlist.
Resources	None necessary
Delivery	Asynchronous delivery through a discussion board forum
Process	In this exercise, learners gain experience in conducting internet searches and sifting through information to locate valuable resources. Using the results of their search, they then create a hotlist or annotated bibliography that is shared with the class.

Post the following instructions:

In this exercise, you will gain expertise in sifting through the vast array of knowledge available on the web to create a "hotlist" of valuable web-based resources. Begin by reviewing information on conducting effective internet searches (add links). Next, using your favorite search engine (list links to popular search engines), locate at least five valuable web-based resources in the form of websites, portals, white papers, or articles on (indicate course topic). Now you are ready to compose your hotlist. For each site that you have located, include:

1. *Title of each web page and its URL*
2. *Two- to four-line annotation about each website that describes the content, key features, and specific information of value. Your annotations should arouse curiosity and motivate readers to visit the sites you have located. Include hyperlinks to all sites and a complete URL address.*

Add a thread to the discussion board forum to post your hotlist.

Evaluation	Hotlists should contain quality sites that provide added knowledge about the course topic. In addition, the annotations that describe the sites should be well written, detailed, and inviting.
Variations	Instead of assigning the entire class to hotlist the general course topic (leadership, diversity, sales, service, etc.), assign each learner a different subtopic for more specific coverage.

The Information Blog

Overview	Learners create and maintain an information blog or weblog that chronicles articles, research, and personal opinion about the course topic.
Objective	Learners conduct internet research, evaluate resources, and compose a weblog of their findings with their personal commentary.
Resources	Weblog host (see Addendum A for ideas)
Delivery	Place instructions in the course assignments section. Create a discussion board forum to house links to learner weblog sites.
Process	Short for weblog, a blog is an online journal that is organized chronologically to provide a running list of commentary and links. It is a web page that can be updated instantly by the user and allows visitors to respond with their comments just as quickly. The information blog is the most common type of weblog. It points to articles, stories, and information all related to a single topic. In this exercise, learners create their own personal information weblogs that correspond to course topic.

Post the following instructions in assignment section:

Here is your chance to develop your own personal presence on the web by creating a blog. The blog, or weblog, is a simple but powerful type of online journal that contains links, stories, and your commentary about a particular topic (include links to popular blogs). *It's easy to design and maintain because new items go on the top and flow down to previous content. Here your blog will address our course topic,* (specify topic). *Here's how to get started. Using a free blog hosting service* (insert links to free sites), *follow the directions to develop your site. Next, conduct a bit of internet research to identify some exciting websites, white papers, portals, and so forth, relating to* (course topic). *Add links to these sites, a brief description, and your commentary. Once your blog is up and running, go to the discussion board forum and add a thread to post the URL for your blog so your fellow classmates can visit. Be sure to update your blog weekly.*

Note: Create a discussion board forum where learners can post URLs for their blogs. You may also want to encourage (or assign) learners to visit the blogs of fellow classmates and add their comments.

Evaluation	Recognize learners for the quality of their links, the value and insight of their commentary, and for visiting and actively participating in the blogs of their classmates.
Variations	Instead of assigning the entire class to weblog the general course topic (leadership, diversity, sales, service, etc.), you might assign each learner a different subtopic for variety.

Inspiring Words

Overview	Each learner identifies and discusses an inspiring quote that relates to the course topic.
Objective	Gain inspiration and motivation from the words of famous leaders.
Resources	Web directories of famous quotes; locate URLs
Delivery	Discussion board forum
Process	Post the following instructions in the discussion board to start a forum: *We can all benefit from a little inspiration. For example, the quote from Albert Einstein, "Imagination is more important than knowledge," reminds me to create courses that allow you to use your creative abilities, rather than overloading you with content. You can find excellent sources for famous and inspiring quotes on the web (provide a few links to get learners started). Locate a quote that relates to our course (leadership, learning, career development, diversity, etc.) and post it here. Also tell us a bit about why you chose that particular quote. How does it inspire you?"*
Evaluation	There is no need to evaluate quotes, but after all are posted, you might ask learners to review this list and vote for their favorite quote. Applaud the originator of the winning quote.
Variations	Follow up with a discussion of how learners can keep inspiring quotes foremost in mind. They might create computer wallpaper that includes the quote, or if your budget allows, you might have the "winning" quote placed on custom mouse pads that you give to each participant.

Link in the Blanks

Overview	Learners "fill in the blanks" in a course-related narrative by adding links to URLs.
Objective	Given an incomplete course-related narrative, learners locate links to sites that contain the appropriate information to fill in the blanks.
Resources	Course-related narrative with incomplete information
Delivery	Asynchronous delivery via discussion board forum
Process	Develop a simple paragraph that deals with course content and ask participants to fill in the blanks with appropriate links or URLs. Create a discussion board forum where learners can post their completed assignments and review the assignments of their classmates. Include the following instructions:
	Review the paragraph below and using your favorite search engine, locate links to sites that contain information that will "fill in the blanks." Blanks must be completed with URLs to sites, not words (see the example that follows).
Evaluation	No evaluation is necessary, but recognize learners for locating interesting, course-related sites.
Variations	Rather than supplying the narrative and blanks, have learners create their own course-related statements that include links to appropriate sites.

Example: Link in the Blanks

In a leadership training course, learners fill in the blanks with links that complete their sentences.

"A prominent past leader who exemplifies the characteristics that I hope to demonstrate is _____. A current leader who I also admire is _____. After looking through many leadership books and publications, the one that most interests me is _____. In putting it all together, the one site that best describes the type of leader that I hope to become is _____."

"A prominent past leader who exemplifies the characteristics that I hope to demonstrate is *http://www.winstonchurchill.org/.*

A current leader who I also admire is *http://www.anc.org.za/people/ mandela. html.* After looking through many leadership books and publications, the one that most interests me is *http://www.josseybass.com/cda/product/0,,0787956783, 00.html.*

In putting it all together, the one site that best describes the type of leader that I hope to become is *http://www.ddiworld.com/products_services/ creatingasericeculture.asp.*"

Note: Rather than typing in words to fill in the blanks, learners locate and include links that provide the answers. When finished, have each participant post their paragraph to the forum so that all may explore their answers and view the linked sites.

Mindmaps

Overview	Use visual software tools to create mindmaps or webs of information, to be used for idea generation, review, or knowledge assessment.
Objective	Given a concept, learners will use mindmapping software to diagram and illustrate knowledge and thoughts.
Resources	Mindmapping software (see Addendum A for recommendations)
Delivery	Asynchronous delivery via discussion board forum
Process	Mindmaps or webs are visual depictions of thoughts and ideas. Mindmaps begin with a central, main concept and branch out with subtopics. Both text and graphics are used to detail the mindmap.

Mindmaps can be used in the beginning of a course to gauge current knowledge, at the end of a course for review, or anytime between to facilitate the processing of information or idea generation. Learners will download software (see Addendum A for recommendations), create mindmaps individually or in groups, and post them to the discussion board.

First, choose a key topic area as the beginning or center of the mindmap. Then provide the following instructions:

Research shows that we can boost our memory and brain function by connecting text with visual images. To facilitate this, we are going to work with mindmaps, a fun and creative way to quickly organize information. First visit (recommended site) and download the free trial software. Review the instructions and samples found on the site to become familiar with the software. Now you are ready to begin mindmapping. Follow these simple guidelines:

1. *Start by placing the key term or principle that you will mindmap (assign key term from course content) at the center of the page and work outward.*
2. *Make the center a clear and strong visual image that depicts the general theme of the map.*
3. *Use color to depict themes and associations, and to highlight areas.*
4. *Use key words and, when possible, add images.*
5. *Use arrows, icons, or other visual aids to show links between different elements.*
6. *Put ideas down as they occur, wherever they fit. Do not judge or hold back.*

When you are finished, post your mindmap to the discussion board forum as an attached file. In your post, include a brief statement about your mindmapping experience. How useful was the exercise? Did you recall more information than expected? Open the mindmaps of fellow learners and review their work. You will need to have the software downloaded on your computer to open the mindmap files. How similar are their maps to yours?

Evaluation

Look for rich detail in mindmaps and extensive use of visual depictions.

Variations

Give learners a skeletal mindmap that contains a key term and four or five main linkages and have them expand the linkages as they review course-related content.

Working in teams, have each group member add four or five linkages to the mindmap and then pass it on (e-mail) to the next member who adds additional linkages, continuing until the mindmap is complete.

Multimedia Scrapbook

Overview	Learners create a multimedia scrapbook that visually represents course topics.
Objective	Using internet resources, learners will locate photos, drawings, graphs, maps, videos, music clips, facts, or quotes and create a visual representation of their course topic.
Resources	Multimedia scrapbook software (see Addendum A for software resources and information about free shareware)
Delivery	Asynchronous discussion board forum
Process	Learners examine and construct knowledge of the course topic from a visual perspective by collecting internet resources in graphic form and compiling them in a multimedia scrapbook. Using free software, learners copy and paste graphic information to a scrapbook and share it with their classmates. Post the following instructions:

You are about to embark on a web-based vacation where you will visit a series of sites that relate to (course topic) and collect photos and souvenirs to help you remember your trip. Next, paste them in a multimedia scrapbook and share your work with the class. Here is your itinerary.

1. *Check out the free multimedia scrapbook software (provide links).*
2. *Search our topic using your favorite search engine, visit interesting sites, and use the cut and paste procedure (provide links and instructions if necessary) to add graphs, cartoons, quotes, maps, or other nontext material to the scrapbook.*
3. *When you are finished, give the scrapbook an appropriate title and post it in our discussion board forum.*

Caution: Check site copyright provisions before downloading graphics. Usually learners are allowed to download images that will be used only in the classroom. Most pages will contain an e-mail link that you may use to write for permission to copy.

Evaluation	Recognize both the quality and quantity of graphic resources that were located.
Variations	Learners add text-based narrative to their scrapbook to summarize the graphic information.

Treasure Hunt

Overview	Learners search a list of sites to locate "buried treasure" in the form of answers to content-related questions.
Objective	Learners review assigned websites and locate the answers to a series of content-related questions.
Resources	Links to websites that contain course information and a series of questions that can be answered with course content
Delivery	Asynchronous delivery via e-mail, discussion board, or online quiz
Process	First conduct a bit of internet research or utilize sites found by your class in the "hotlist" project, to identify web pages that contain information essential to your course topic. Gather web page links (not just the website, but the actual page URL within the site). Next, formulate one question that can be answered by each link. You may send the assignment by e-mail, post it in your course assignment section, or create an objective quiz that contains the questions to be answered. Post the following instructions:
	You will visit some important internet sites and practice your research skills by searching for "buried treasure" in the form of answers to course-related questions. Each question comes with a link to a web page that contains its answer. Visit the page, quickly find the answer, and move ahead to locate all the treasure. (Add directions for posting answers.)
Evaluation	Recognize learners who provide accurate answers.
Variations	Instead of delivering this as a single assignment, create a question of the day or week and spread the contest out throughout the course.

True or False

Overview	Learners post statements about the course content that may or may not be true. Classmates guess the accuracy of the statements, supporting their guesses with references to class materials or online resources.
Objective	Learners first construct and post statements about course content and then evaluate the accuracy of statements posted by their classmates.
Resources	None necessary
Delivery	Asynchronous discussion board forum
Process	In the discussion board, each learner posts a content-related statement. Other learners must decide whether the statement is true or false and post links or references to course material to back up their decision. Create a discussion board forum with the following instructions:

> *Post a statement about an aspect of our course material. Your statement can be either true or false and should require a bit of research to determine its accuracy. Next, review the statements posted by your fellow classmates and take a guess as to whether you think their statements are true or false. Back up your guess with references from your course material or an online source. Check your statement frequently and when someone guesses correctly, add a thread to their post to let them know they are correct. Keep making guesses until questions have been answered correctly.*

Evaluation	Recognize those learners who make the most correct guesses.
Variations	Add detail to the exercise by asking each learner to post three statements, one that is true and two that are false. Classmates follow up with posts where they attempt to identify the true statement.

Twenty Questions

Overview	Each learner thinks of a course-related term and classmates guess what it is by asking questions with "yes" or "no" answers.
Objective	Given course-related material, learners formulate questions and distinguish between terminology.
Resources	None necessary
Delivery	Asynchronous discussion board forum
Process	Create a discussion board forum with the following instructions:

> *To review the course material, we will play an online version of an old favorite, twenty questions. First, think of a course-related term. Add a thread to this forum that says: "This is (your name). Can you guess what I am thinking of?" When everyone in class has added their individual thread, return to the board and play the game. Ask your classmates questions that can be answered by "yes" or "no" to guess the term or concept that each is thinking of. As soon as you think you know the secret term, take a guess. Make only one guess per thread or per classmate. Your thread ends when twenty (or you might choose to shorten the game by making it ten) questions have been asked or when the correct term has been guessed.*

Note: For this game to work, learners must log on to the discussion board for a few minutes each day to respond to posted questions. If this is not feasible, you might play out the game during a longer period of time by starting early in the course and letting it run throughout the delivery period.

Evaluation	Recognize those learners who make the most correct guesses and those whose term achieved twenty questions or were the most difficult to guess.
Variations	Rather than having each learner create his or her own game within the forum, present a single term and instruct the class members to ask twenty questions about this term only. The game can be continued with the addition of new terms.

Virtual Field Trip

Overview	Learners embark on a virtual field trip where they explore visually appealing sites that support course content.
Objective	Given a virtual field trip excursion, learners will visualize and recall content-based information.
Resources	Virtual field trip embedded in course content (see software recommendations in Addendum A)
Delivery	Asynchronous delivery
Process	Develop a virtual field trip using recommended software (see software resources for free downloads and trials in Addendum A). Virtual field trips allow viewers to scroll through various linked web pages and read text-based commentary so they might expand their horizons without leaving the course site.
	Select a topic that is aligned with your course objectives and contains visual appeal (cultural diversity, tour of competitors, best practices, corporate orientation) and locate web-based visual resources (scanned photos, web graphics, etc.). Add text narration and important facts.
Evaluation	Use objective test to measure recall of field trip content.
Variations	Assign learners, either individually or in teams, to create virtual field trips as course projects.

Webquest

Overview	A dynamic, web-based activity that involves research, critical thinking, and evaluation.
Objective	Given a Webquest,[42] learners will explore and evaluate new information on the web and clearly communicate their conclusions.
Resources	A Webquest embedded in a course assignment with discussion board forum
Delivery	Asynchronous delivery
Process	Design a Webquest to explore a key component of your course. The Webquest will allow learners to examine web-based resources, critically examine a key aspect of the course topic, and communicate their analysis to the class. Learners may work individually or in groups to complete webquests (see guidelines for creating Webquests following this activity and also the sample Webquest). Follow up with a discussion board forum where learners can post and discuss the completed assignment.
Evaluation	Recognize learners who achieve the goals of the Webquest, create thoughtful analyses, and formulate detailed reports.
Variations	Ask learners to create mini Webquests themselves, post them to the discussion board, and choose one or two peer developed Webquests to complete.

Designing Webquests

Step 1:   Choose a topic that relates directly to your course objectives.

Step 2:   Select an authentic task that will demonstrate higher thinking skills.

Step 3:   Locate web-based resources for your Webquest.

Step 4:   Create the Webquest and include the following:

1. An introduction that sets the stage and explains the purpose of the Webquest
2. A "road map"or list of websites or locations that learners should explore
3. A task that is doable and interesting and that records and communicates the results of the quest
4. A description of the process the learners should follow as they locate and review information (What key questions should they consider as they review the links?)
5. Details about your grading process (What are the characteristics of excellent Webquest assignments?)
6. A conclusion that brings closure to the quest, reminds learners of the task to be completed, and explains how it might be communicated

Step 5:   Deliver the Webquest as a paper-based assignment, web page, or Power-Point presentation.

Sample Webquest

Webquest 4: Are You Ready to be an E-Trainer?

In this Webquest, you will do the following:

♦ Explore careers in e-training
♦ Explore your strengths and weaknesses
♦ Determine if e-training is the right career for you

You may be wondering what it is like to be an e-trainer. Training at a distance is certainly different than classroom delivery. Review *The Life and Times of an E-Trainer* to learn more about the trials and tribulations of virtual training delivery. Still sound interesting? The next step is to assess your particular readiness for distance learning design and delivery. Review the article, "E-Learning Competencies," and critically compare your current abilities to those identified for an e-trainer.

It's your turn. Search the internet by using search engines such as *http://www.google.com/* and *http://www.lycos.com/* to locate additional information about careers in e-training. Be sure to make note of the web-sites and articles you locate.

Now it is time to analyze and evaluate the information you have col-lected. Write a one-page summary of your findings. Excellent Webquests will contain the following:

◆ Your thoughts on e-learning and e-training
◆ Description of your current e-training competencies
◆ Summary of the competencies you need to develop or fine-tune if you want to become (or progress as) an e-trainer
◆ Plan for your development—how you will learn what you need to know
◆ List of additional websites and articles you found helpful in your decision

Post your summary to the group discussion board as a response to my post. Read the posts of fellow group members, ask questions, and provide support.

CHAPTER 8
Group Discussion

In group discussion, learners explore issues and topics relating to the course content, express opinions, draw upon prior knowledge, and often construct new knowledge based on interaction with peers. Using available technology, this valuable experience can be reconstructed online, sometimes even more effectively than in traditional settings. In virtual discussion, cultural and personal biases are less important, and reticent participants may communicate freely, particularly if discussions are designed so that all must participate. On the other hand, some learners may find virtual communication intimidating and may require additional get-to-know-you exercises at the start or greater encouragement from the facilitator to participate.

In an e-learning discussion, a written transcript is made so that learners and trainers can refer to the interaction at a later date. On the down side, it may be more difficult to manage conflict without face-to-face contact and those who have difficulty expressing themselves in print will not perform as well. In most situations, the advantages offered by the increased interactivity that results from group discussion far outweigh the disadvantages.

Group discussion can occur either asynchronously or synchronously. Asynchronous communication allows us to move beyond the confines of scheduling so trainers and learners may interact at their convenience. Communication does not take place in real time, allowing maximum flexibility and freedom of use. Added benefits are learners have time to research and reflect on their responses and global communication is possible without time zone constraint.

Synchronous e-learning requires that all parties are online simultaneously. Synchronous interaction allows for immediate feedback and enhanced social interaction. It more accurately approximates communication in the classroom where time restraints govern the frequency and length of interaction. The disadvantages of synchronous training include scheduling difficulties that occur when all parties must be at their computers and ready to learn simultaneously, and the need to limit class size to allow the facilitator to adequately address individual learners.

The group discussion exercises that follow can be delivered either synchronously through live chat or asynchronously via your delivery system's discussion or bulletin board, depending on the needs of your learners and the size of your class.

Jigsaw

Overview	This virtual jigsaw exercise allows learners to discuss and share information in teams.
Objective	Learners develop expertise in a course topic in their home team, and then share that knowledge with their learning team.
Resources	Listing of team assignments to both the home team and the learning team
Delivery	Synchronous chat, asynchronous discussion board, or e-mail
Process	Place learners in a home team where they share course-related knowledge about a specific topic or component of a topic via online chat, e-mail, or group discussion board. Each team is assigned a different topic, so if there are four home teams, there are four different topics. Next, rearrange teams so that the homogenous groups or home teams are organized into new heterogeneous groups or learning teams that consist of one or more representatives from each new topic area. Provide the following instructions:

> *This is a jigsaw exercise where you will first be placed in a home team and assigned a topic to explore as a group. As a group, you will use your course content and the web to develop expertise in your particular topic. Next, I will rearrange or "jigsaw" everyone into learning teams. Here you will meet with a new group of classmates, each being experts on a different topic. You will teach your topic to your new group, sharing all the information you have acquired in your home team. (Specify how you might want learners to teach their new team—discussion board post, PowerPoint slides, mindmap, live chat, e-mail, creation of a website, etc.) Your new team members will teach you their specialty topics, so you will benefit from all the information gathered by each of the home teams.*

Evaluation	Follow up with a quiz or assignment that is based on the content.
Variations	Encourage learners to develop creative, practice-based ways to teach their information to their new group. Rather than just conveying text-based information, ask that they deliver their content in an active, experiential manner.

Process Facilitation

Overview	In teams, learners take on roles to facilitate either synchronous or asynchronous discussion.
Objective	Contribute to online discussion by demonstrating assigned responsibilities in group facilitation and process.
Resources	None necessary
Delivery	Asynchronous discussion board forum or synchronous chat
Process	Assign learners to groups and provide a course-related topic for discussion. The process for the exercise is as follows:

1. Select a topic for discussion. The topic you choose should facilitate the exploration of varying points of view and require that a decision be made about the group's position. For example, in a "Train the Trainer" course, groups discuss various theories of adult learning and select the one theory they believe best enhances adult learning. In a course addressing multiculturalism, groups decide whether it is possible to change the beliefs that we have about different cultures and, if so, how this change process might be implemented.
2. Assign learners to groups of four to eight people.
3. Develop process roles for each group member to ensure successful group process management (see "Group Roles" following this activity for recommendations).

Provide the following instructions:

> *You will both participate in an online discussion of* (assigned topic) *and also take on specific responsibilities to manage your group process. Please see the attached list of roles and note your assignment and the responsibilities you will have for making sure the group works well together.* (Provide list and assign each group member to a role.)
>
> *Next, log on to the online chat* (synchronous delivery, include date and time) *or visit the discussion board forum* (asynchronous delivery) *and begin to discuss your ideas regarding the topic. The initiator will begin the process by making the first post or comment.*
>
> *In addition to presenting your ideas about the topic, facilitate the process by responding to the ideas of others "in role."*

Evaluation	Assign one member (most likely the summarizer) to share the group's conclusions with the remainder of the class by making a post to the general forum.
Variations	Rather than assigning a topic, allow groups to select their own topic for discussion, making the choice of the topic part of the group process.

Group Roles

The **initiator** gets the team started by asking an initial question such as, "How should we approach this task?" Agreeing on a game plan before starting the task is crucial to team effectiveness and is the distinguishing characteristic of the initiator.

The **summarizer** urges the group to acknowledge consensus and reach a decision. By briefly reflecting the discussion that has taken place thus far, the summarizer asks for agreement and suggests that the group move on to the next step.

The **orienter** prevents the team from wandering too far from the topic at hand; he or she brings the team back in focus when astray. Redirecting is not abrupt, but is accomplished in a neutral fashion with a question such as, "Are we off topic right now?"

The **fact seeker** identifies gaps in information necessary to make a sound decision. The fact seeker may suggest that the team acquire additional data before proceeding and organize the collection of data.

The **harmonizer** recognizes conflict and directs the group to take steps to resolve issues. The harmonizer helps the team recognize the value of different points of view so that group members can better understand each other's perspective.

The **gatekeeper** tracks group communication and participation. The gatekeeper ensures that all team members actively listen to each other and understand the others' messages. The gatekeeper paraphrases messages so that everyone is understood, and invites quieter members to participate while ensuring that active members do not dominate the discussion.

The **encourager** builds and sustains team energy by showing support for people's efforts, ideas, and achievements. The encourager emphasizes members' participation by giving verbal approval such as "Good point—that's a great idea!"

The Projector and Screen

Overview   Learners examine course-related problems or issues that are presented by the "projector" with both positive and negative consequences reflected in the "screens."

Objective   Learners first identify a course-related problem or issue, analyze it in terms of both positive and negative outcomes, and choose the best course of action.

Resources   None necessary

Delivery   Synchronous chat or asynchronous discussion board forum

Process   In groups of three, one member acts as the "projector" and presents a content-based problem, while the other two members act as either the positive or negative "screens" reflecting the possible outcomes. Assign learners to groups of three and instruct them to carry out the exercise either asynchronously in the discussion board or synchronously in a private chat. Include the following directions.

This communication exercise allows you to examine issues or problems from different points of view. You will be assigned to one of three roles:

Projector: Identifies a work-based, course content–related issue for analysis that involves a decision, choice, or change (should we outsource, enter new markets, expand our diversity initiative, etc.?). *Describes the issue in detail and ask for reactions from your partners.*

Positive screen: Presents potential positive outcomes of the action. Reflects a rosy view of possible outcomes resulting from the change.

Negative screen: Reflects the negative aspects of the issue. Presents the dark side of the issue or choice. You will meet (instructor chooses synchronous or asynchronous delivery) *to present the issue and reflect possible outcomes. When the dialogue is complete and both "screens" have reflected their positions, the "projector" will summarize the results and make a decision, communicating the rationale for the choice.*

Evaluation   Look for detailed problem development from the "projector" and much dialogue and idea generation from the "screens."

Variations   Learners chart or mindmap their discussion by developing a diagram with the problem in the middle and the positive and negative screens on each side.

The Virtual Fishbowl

Overview	Total class involvement in live chat can become chaotic. In the virtual fishbowl, half the class participates actively in a live chat while the others tune in and observe.
Objective	Discuss and debate a course-related topic, then provide feedback and observations.
Resources	A topic and a teacher-developed list of open-ended questions for discussion (based on course content)
Delivery	Synchronous delivery via live chat
Process	If you have a large class, you may need to schedule more than one "fishbowl" to accommodate discussion groups of eight to ten people. Post the following instructions, a list of questions that will be asked during the fishbowl, and the fishbowl group assignments.

> *In a fishbowl exercise, one group discusses a topic (in the fishbowl so to speak) while the other group observes the discussion. We are going to take part in a virtual fishbowl during a live chat. Half the class will participate in an online discussion while the other half observes without participating.*

Note: The learners in the fishbowl become a small class in the midst of a large one. When we're finished, the observers will provide insight and feedback. Please see the attached topic and questions that we will be discussing during our live event. Look them over and be prepared to participate.

When the fishbowl discussion ends, ask for feedback from the observers.

Evaluation	Recognize the first group or "fishbowl" for their active participation in the discussion and thoughtful answers. Also recognize the second group for their keen observations and feedback.
Variations	The fishbowl can also take place asynchronously in a forum, where one group participates in an active asynchronous discussion and a second group of learners review the discussion and provide summary and feedback.

CHAPTER 9
Idea Generation

Brainstorming activities allow learners to quickly develop and communicate new ideas for product development, process revision, and problem resolution. Brainstorming exercises can be implemented in almost all training and course delivery and are a great way to get e-learners involved. In brainstorming, participants are supplied with new data and fresh ideas by quickly tapping a broad spectrum of opinion and expertise. Most learners enjoy the freedom of expression inherent in brainstorming. Solutions to previously insoluble problems can be discovered and all members of the group can be encouraged to participate.

Electronic delivery provides excellent opportunity for brainstorming, consensus building, and idea generation. The activities that follow can be delivered via e-mail, asynchronous discussion board, or live chat. Ideas and thoughts can be quickly posted on a course site for everyone to see and evaluate. Please note synchronous brainstorming requires quick response and is best completed on computers with fast internet connection.

Brainwriting

Overview	Brainwriting is a brainstorming or creativity exercise that involves the written generation of alternatives in a group setting.
Objective	Build on the thoughts of others to develop a series of alternative ideas.
Resources	E-mail distribution list
Delivery	E-mail
Process	Develop a brainwriting topic or question based on your course content (How can we ensure that our customers return? How can we better serve our markets? How can we improve our operation?). The process assumes that you have completed a thorough diagnosis of a problem and want to generate alternative solutions. Start the brainwriting session by sending the following e-mail message to all learners.

> *We are going to use a written creativity technique called brainwriting to generate a list of alternatives to our dilemma. Here is the problem we face: (include your brainwriting topic here). The first person on our distribution list (note the person's name) will start us off by thinking of one or two solutions to solve this problem. She (or he) will forward these ideas, along with my original message, to the next person on the list who will add one or two additional solutions, then forward it to the next person, and so on, until we have a long list of solutions to our problem. The last person on the list (include name) will then forward the completed list to me and I will post it to our bulletin board so all can see your great ideas. You have 24 hours from the receipt of the e-mail to open it, add to it, and forward it. You have three choices when you receive the e-mail: You can add to the ideas of others, come up with a new idea of your own, or pass the e-mail to the next person.*

Evaluation	All ideas are valuable in brainwriting so no formal evaluation is needed. After posting the ideas to the board, you might ask learners to vote for their favorite idea. Keep the topic alive for your learners by asking them to elaborate on how they might implement alternatives.
Variations	If time is short, rather than forwarding ideas, you might ask learners to generate ideas or solutions and e-mail them directly to you. Then develop a list of ideas and post them on the board, followed by a vote for the favorite as described above.

Defining Excellence

Overview	Learners generate definitions of *excellence* as it relates to the topic under study and provide examples of best practices that demonstrate those qualities.
Objective	Given the course topic, learners first formulate their personal definition of *excellence* and then select several examples that demonstrate excellence.
Resources	None necessary
Delivery	Asynchronous discussion board forum
Process	Select a topic that represents the essence of your course (e.g., service, leadership, communication, multiculturalism). Create a forum in the discussion board with the following instructions.

> *Here we will create a personal definition of excellence in terms of* (course topic). *First think about what excellent* (course topic) *means to you personally. Then post a list of several characteristics that come to mind. Finally, locate at least three web-based resources that demonstrate the excellent qualities you have listed. These could be links to organizations, websites, articles, products, or services. Post the URL for the link next to the characteristic that it embodies.*

Evaluation	Recognize learners for the detail they provide in their definitions of excellence and the appropriateness of the web-based resources they locate. In your feedback, let them know that you have "heard" them and that you "spent time with" their ideas. There is no greater praise for students than to have a respected individual take their ideas seriously.
Variations	Instead of working individually, have learners work in groups to develop their definitions in a synchronous chat or group-only forum.
	Create a master definition of your topic by tallying the characteristics of excellence that your learners provide in their posts. Create a final post that lists the top five or ten characteristics of excellence.

E-storming

Overview	This e-mail-based, idea-generating process involves both class members and their associates.
Objective	Generate a wide assortment of ideas by expanding to include a diverse group external to the course.
Resources	None necessary
Delivery	E-mail and asynchronous discussion board forum
Process	In this activity, ideas are not generated by your learners, but by their friends, co-workers, and associates. Begin by posing a question or topic for consideration (much like that in the brainwriting exercise). Next, send the following instructions to your class.

> *You will have the opportunity to participate in one of the newest virtual creativity techniques, called e-storming, which involves the generation of ideas and solutions from a broad, diverse audience via e-mail. Instead of generating solutions or ideas yourself, you will forward the topic or question under consideration (describe topic or question here) to at least five of your friends, co-workers, or associates and ask them to send you their thoughts and solutions. Be sure to explain that this is a class project and that all ideas and solutions are acceptable. Remember Linus Pauling's words, "The best way to have a good idea is to have lots of ideas."*
>
> *Next, compile a list of all the ideas and solutions and e-mail them to me (give time period for assignment here). I will then post them to our board for everyone to share.*

Evaluation	All ideas in e-storming are viable, so no formal evaluation is needed. After posting the ideas to the board, you might ask learners to vote for their favorite idea.
Variations	Learners might send their requests for ideas to experts or leaders in the field. Responses might be fewer, but those that you do receive should be quite valuable.

Top Ten Lists

Overview	This quick way to poll opinion uses virtual tools to create and communicate content-related top ten lists.
Objective	Given a topic, learners provide opinions and ideas that are formulated into consensus through the creation of a top ten list.
Resources	Course content
Delivery	Asynchronous via e-mail and discussion board forum
Process	David Letterman has made the top ten list legendary in popular culture. Here you will involve your class in developing a combined top ten list that relates to your course content. Identify a topic for your list (Top 10 Errors, Top 10 Best Practices, Top Ten Theorists, etc.) and send each class member the following instructions in an e-mail.

We are going to create a top ten list of (title). *Each class member will e-mail me their favorite practices* (one or two entries) *that relate to our particular topic. I will tally the votes and develop an all-time top ten list for the class so we can see where we stand as a group. Look for the class top ten list on our course site next week. So jot down your top ten picks and e-mail them to me by* (due date).

Note: Tally the answers and create a top ten list in the style of David Letterman that begins with the tenth most popular item and ends with the first or most popular item. Post this on the discussion board or in the course announcement section.

Evaluation	Recognize learners for their participation.
Variations	E-mail consensus games[43] can also be used to quickly gage opinion or gain feedback about the course. Ask trainees to send their top ten picks for what they have learned during the semester, such as top ten most memorable course experiences or top ten ideas they will use back on the job.

CHAPTER 10
Closers

The way your e-learning course ends is just as important as the way it begins. Just as you would not end a traditional course by saying, "That's it. We're done. Goodbye," e-learning delivery must also contain a bit of ceremony at the end. Closers allow learners to revisit the course, record their ideas, and provide a link to the workplace. Your learners have worked hard during the course to form relationships and master content. Closers give them an opportunity to reinforce learning, say goodbye, provide feedback, and create a plan for the future. The following exercises offer ideas for effective endings to e-learning courses. When selecting a closer, consider the characteristics of both your learners and your objectives. In courses that were content driven, a closing exercise that incorporates review might be most appropriate. When close relationships were formed through collaborative learning, closing exercises might be more interactive and focus on providing feedback and future support. In any event, look for opportunities to promote transfer to the workplace through goal development and follow-up.

Electronic Yearbook

Overview	Learners sign an electronic "yearbook" as a closing exercise.
Objective	To provide positive feedback to classmates, learners post comments and closing remarks to each other in their site guest books.
Resources	Individual learner websites or web pages with guest book (see Addendum A for free guest book services), class list of URLs for individual sites
Delivery	Asynchronous delivery
Process	Create an electronic "yearbook" that trainees sign at the end of a program. Include comments that encourage, provide positive feedback, and recall course-related experiences. Learners create simple web pages or blogs about themselves or use existing web pages (see the "Blogging" [Chapters 4 and 7] exercises). Make sure that each has a "guest book" function. Guestbooks let visitors add comments and remarks to your site. (See Addendum A for recommended free guest book software.) Provide the following instructions in your assignment section: *Visit the websites of each of your classmates and imagine that you are signing their "yearbook." Using their guest book, add positive comments and thoughts about your experiences with the class and with that particular individual. Visit your own site and read comments from classmates who signed your guest book.*
Evaluation	Ask learners to copy you on all the comments they have posted. Create a master list of comments and look for common experiences.
Variations	Create an online survey where trainees vote or nominate fellow learners for such awards as Most Congenial, Most Likely to Take Another E-Learning Course, and Best Online Attendance. Post the results.

E-mail Check-up

Overview	Learners create goal statements for future performance at the end of a training program. The trainer tracks progress with electronic follow-up.
Objective	To facilitate transfer, upon completion of the course, learners construct goals for future performance based on course content. The trainer follows up electronically to track progress.
Resources	None necessary
Delivery	E-mail
Process	Learners send the instructor an e-mail that contains three changes they plan to implement when they return to the workplace. The instructor saves the e-mail, and at thirty- and sixty-day intervals, sends it back to the learner to check progress. Provide the following instructions:

> *Now that you have completed this course, think about three changes you plan to make back on the job* (or goals to be accomplished). *Be specific about what you will do, how you will do it, and when it will be accomplished. Send me an e-mail detailing these changes and your plans for implementing them. I will hold this e-mail and send it back to you* (specify time interval) *so you can see your progression.*

Evaluation	Applaud learners for progress toward achieving their goals. When learners have failed to make progress, continue e-mail dialogue to coach them toward improved performance.
Variations	Consider having learners develop goal statements at the start of the course, review their accomplishment at the end of the course, and revise them for transfer to future courses or the workplace.
	Copy the learner's supervisor on both the goal statement and follow-up communication.

Time Capsule

Overview	Learners create a virtual time capsule filled with testimonials and valuable advice for future trainees.
Objective	Upon completion of the course, learners assess their experience and construct a series of positive comments about the course and identify strategies that might help future learners.
Resources	None necessary
Delivery	E-mail
Process	Create a virtual time capsule to pass on to future learners so they might see how others have successfully completed the course. Provide the following instructions.

We are going to create a "virtual time capsule" to pass on to future learners who take this course. In this time capsule will be your positive experiences with the course material and interaction, strategies that helped you successfully complete the course, and any ideas or suggestions you have for future learners as they start out. Think about information that might have helped you when you began this class. E-mail your comments and suggestions to me and I will combine comments from the entire class and create a virtual time capsule to be opened by future learners as they begin this course. I will also post the time capsule (note location of post) so you may see the comments and suggestions from your class.

Evaluation	Recognize learners for contributing to the time capsule. Also note that the comments you receive are valuable for future course design and revision.
Variations	Have a "virtual reunion" six months or one year after the course and have learners open their time capsule.
	Ask learners to also add the web resources and sites that they found most useful. Include these links in the time capsule for future learners to use.

Virtual Cruise

Overview	This ending activity allows learners to give and receive feedback about their "online identities" by playing the cruise ship game.
Objective	Learners provide feedback to their classmates by specifying the roles they believe each member would have on a cruise ship.
Resources	None necessary
Delivery	Asynchronous discussion board forum
Process	Learners identify the roles they would see their fellow classmates taking if they were all on a cruise ship together. This requires two forums. In the first forum, learners post roles for each classmate. In the second forum, learners react to the roles they have been assigned. Either carry out this exercise with the entire class or in groups if your class is large (more than twenty people). Post the following directions in the first forum.

> *Imagine that you are all on a Caribbean cruise together. Tell us which roles you see your fellow classmates playing on the cruise. Some might have specific job responsibilities (captain, doctor, activities director, etc.) or be a guest (describe characteristics, e.g., writer looking for new material, person hoping to escape problems, just looking for fun). Post a brief description for each class member (or group member).*
>
> *Next, look over the posts and in the second forum, tell us whether you agree with the way your classmates view you.*

Post the following question in the second forum:

> *How does your online personality differ from the way you come across in person?*

Evaluation	Recognize learners who provide detailed analyses of their online personas.
Variations	Ask learners to indicate the position they see themselves holding on the cruise ship. How does this differ from their classmates' perceptions?

Virtual Reunion

Overview	Learners participate in a virtual class reunion at a later date where they discuss transfer success.
Objective	At a set period following course completion, learners communicate their success in achieving transfer of course skills and knowledge.
Resources	None necessary
Delivery	Asynchronous or synchronous delivery
Process	One month after their course ends, learners participate in either a synchronous chat or asynchronous discussion board forum where they describe their successes and failures in transfer of the knowledge and skill from their class to their workplace. Provide the following instructions. *You won't need to lose weight or don cocktail attire for this reunion. We're going to meet virtually, one month after our class ends, to celebrate or commiserate about your posttraining experiences with this course. We'll talk about how readily the skills and knowledge you developed transferred to your job. I'll send you a special e-mail invitation to the event, so you can be sure to put it on your calendar.*
Evaluation	Recognize those who achieved successful transfer and facilitate the development of additional transfer strategies for those who were not successful.
Variations	After the reunion, create a list of the ten best transfer strategies based on class input and forward it to all past learners.

ADDENDUM A
Recommended Freeware and Software Trials

The following software resources facilitate the delivery of some activities included in this book. They are tried and tested sources. All are either freeware or offer free trials (at the time of writing), allowing your learners to complete the course activity without purchasing additional resources. Some resources are more difficult than others to use, so try to download and practice them yourself so you accurately gage your learners' ability to master them.

Virtual Greeting Cards

Postcard Place
A wide array of virtual greetings
http://www.postcardplace.com

MIT Media Lab
Virtual postcards featuring fine art
http://persona.www.media.mit.edu/Postcards/cardrack.html

Weblog Hosting
Salon
Radio Userland Software free 30-day trial download
http://www.salon.com/blogs/downloads/index.html

Blogger
Free hosting
http://www.blogger.com

Desktop Collaboration
Groove
Outstanding collaboration software: free download for personal use or 90-day
   business trial
http://www.groove.net/downloads/groove/index.gtml

MOOs

enCore Xpress
Free MOO development software download from University of Texas at Dallas
http://lingua.utdallas.edu/encore

Tapped In
Free software download for MOO development
http://www.tappedin.org

Visual Diagramming

Inspiration
Outstanding mindmapping software: 30-day trial
http://www.inspiration.com/freetrial/index.cfm?fuseaction5insp

IHMC Concept Map Software
Free concept mapping software for educational use
http://cmap.coginst.uwf.edu

Smartdraw
Free 30-day trial of mindmapping/concept mapping software
http://www.smartdraw.com/downloads/index.htm

Digital Photo Album

Kodak's Ofoto
Free site that allows you to create and share virtual photo albums
http://www.ofoto.com

Smartdraw Photo
Free software to create and organize photos
http://www.smartdraw.com/specials/photo-album.asp?id524179

Storyboarding

Atomic Learning
Free storyboard software
http://www.atomiclearning.com/freestoryboard.shtml

Writer's Blocks
Free trial: story development software
http://www.writersblocks.com/trial.htm

Multimedia Scrapbooks

Paint Shop Photo Album 4
See the free trial
http://www.jasc.com/products/trialreg.asp?pid=K-PSPA4-USDIR

The following is a scrapbooking tutorial for Paint Shop Photo Album 4:
http://www.jasc.com/support/learn/tutorials/paintshoppro/207scrapbook.asp?

Virtual Field Trips

Tramline
Trial version of Tourmaker creates virtual field trips
http://www.field-guides.com/tm/download.htm

Utah Education Network
Free software for virtual tours
http://www.uen.org/utahlink/tours

Guest Books

Aborior's Guestbook Application
Free software that creates a guestbook for your visitors to sign, comment on
    your site, or just say hello
http://www.aborior.com/simplex/lite.shtml

Visitorbook Pro
Free version of guestbook software
http://www.visitorbook.com/downloads

Virtual Meetings

Centra E-meeting Software
Free 30-day trial that allows you to hold virtual meetings
https://www.centranow.com/registration/register.asp

Net Meeting
Microsoft Internet Explorer's (version 4.0 and higher) built-in conferencing
    program, called NetMeeting: free download of the most recent version and
    instructions on use
http://www.microsoft.com/windows/netmeeting

Miscellaneous Free Software Trials

ZD Net
Information on free trials on an array of software
http://downloads-zdnet.com.com/2001-20-0.html

CNET.com
Search for free software in shareware
http://shareware.cnet.com

ADDENDUM B
E-Learning Design Checklist

The following criteria are evident in quality e-learning courses.

Course Appearance

Page backgrounds are white or pale pastel with contrasting text colors and graphics.

Fonts are easy to read in both on-screen and printed versions.

Page size is at or near a standard 800×600 pixel resolution.

Screens take advantage of white space to display information on the page.

Graphics occupy minimum screen space and are used only to enhance the content.

Graphics file sizes are minimized for rapid loading.

Navigation

Site navigation is clearly specified so learners know where to find information.

Hyperlinks are attached to a few key words or a meaningful phrase.

Links and URLs are unambiguous, clear, and specific, and they are as brief as possible.

Backward links are provided so that learners can return to their starting place.

Links to all software required for assignments and course completion are included.

Access to reference materials or a knowledge base for independent research is provided.

Module Design

Course material is written in an active voice using first or second person and a conversational style.

All text is grammatically correct.

Assignments and projects are clearly described and include examples.

Learning objectives are clearly stated and describe the specific knowledge, skills, and abilities that learners will develop.

Each assignment, learning activity, or post is directly tied to a learning objective.

Each learning module includes an opportunity for the learner to practice and demonstrate acceptable performance and receive feedback.

Material is chunked in modules to facilitate retention.

Design contains diverse interactivity opportunities that challenge learners.

Design includes examples that are supported by analogies, metaphors, and stories.

Content needed most often is in a prominent place.

Practice exercises include links that describe their theoretical or conceptual basis.

Design stimulates and facilitates collaboration with fellow learners.

Delivery

Course media requirements are consistent with software and hardware available to learners.

Ready access is provided to course instructor or mentor for quick response to questions.

Progress and success are measured and tracked.

Engagement techniques are used to motivate learners.

Includes feedback from the instructor, peers, and self.

Rapid turnaround time on all assignments is provided.

ADDENDUM C
Creating and Delivering E-Learning Games

The following checklist will help you to adapt and create e-learning games that fit the needs of your learners and your course material. Keep in mind that the most successful games or activities are linked directly to the achievement of course objectives.

Prepare

Here you will gather information and resources to help you plan for your delivery.

_____ 1. Select one course objective.

_____ 2. Assess the skill level of your audience. Consider both the content-related expertise and technological know-how.

_____ 3. Consider Bloom's taxonomy of learning (Table C.1) and identify the cognitive domain that you wish to address.

_____ 4. Identify how you would achieve this in traditional delivery—lecture, group discussion, quiz, etc.

_____ 5. Identify web resources that you have available—test creation, discussion board, e-mail, video, audio, chat, etc.

Design

In this phase, you will create the learning activity. Begin by thinking about how you would teach this segment traditionally. Next consider resources that would facilitate delivery in a web-based environment.

_____ 6. Briefly describe your learning activity. Give it a catchy title.

_____ 7. Write the objectives. What do you want learners to accomplish? Base this on your course objective.

_____ 8. List the resources that learners will need.

_____ 9. Identify the delivery mode.

_____ 10. Make it fun. Identify novel ways to deliver or introduce the learning activity to gain attention and add interest.

_____ 11. Add some WIFM (what's in it for me). Let learners know how they will benefit from this activity. If appropriate, link expertise to workplace performance.

_____ 12. Describe the process. Write detailed instructions and review them several times for accuracy.

_____ 13. Develop debriefing questions or comments.

Deliver

Collect formative assessment by having subject matter experts or colleagues evaluate the game. Based on feedback, make revisions as necessary.

_____ 14. Pilot the game by delivering it to colleagues or individual learners.

_____ 15. Revise as needed.

_____ 16. Deliver the learning activity synchronously or asynchronously.

_____ 17. Be available to answer questions and provide encouragement.

Assess

_____ 18. Identify a standard against which you will assess performance (worked example, rubric, checklist).

_____ 19. Deliver feedback individually to participants based on the standard of performance.

_____ 20. Check reaction. Ask learners for their opinion about the success of the game.

Table C.1
Bloom's Taxonomy[1]

Benjamin Bloom created a taxonomy of intellectual behavior important in learning. The cognitive domain involves the acquisition and use of knowledge and is predominant in the majority of courses. Bloom identified six levels within the cognitive domain, with knowledge being the most simplistic and evaluation the most advanced.

Cognitive Domain	Skills Demonstrated	Corresponding Learning Activities
Knowledge	The learner is able to recall, restate, and remember learned information.	Tests, quizzes, recall games
Comprehension	The learner grasps the meaning of information by interpreting and translating what has been learned.	Explain, interpret, or rephrase
Application	The learner uses the new information in a context different from the one in which it was learned.	Locate examples, create a model or visual diagram of existing material
Analysis	The learner separates the material, situation, or environment into its component parts and focuses on the relationships among these parts.	Divide into subtopics, compare and contrast with other topics, gather opinions, classify, draw conclusions
Synthesis	The learner creates new information with what has been learned.	Make predictions, create a new process, develop a new model, identify new ways to use information
Evaluation	The learner makes judgments about new information on the basis of established criteria.	Order information based on importance, critically evaluate information, identify potential shortcomings, recommend improvements, provide opinions

[1]B. Bloom, *Taxonomy of Educational Objectives: The Classification of Educational Goals* (New York: McKay, 1956).

ADDENDUM D
Examples of Learning Activities

Forum: A Definition of Training Excellence

The following instructions are posted in the discussion board to create a forum.

Here we will create a personal definition of excellence in terms of training. First think about what excellent training means to you personally. Then post a list of several characteristics that come to mind. Finally, locate at least one web-based resource that demonstrates the excellent qualities you have listed. These could be links to organizations, websites, articles, products, or services. Post the URL for the link next to the characteristic that it embodies.

Learner 1 Post

I found this post to be most challenging.

After years in the field of training and development, I have been given the opportunity to work with excellent trainers and developers. Over the years, I have learned to identify patterns in their behavior. In fact, I have spent a great deal of time thinking about these patterns and the individual characteristics that I admire, emulate, and deem necessary in the profession. Enclosed are my characteristics and links to support them.

1. Passion and vision
    http://www.dewittjones.com/html/extraordinary.shtml
2. Ability to build positive relationships
    http://www.blanchardtraining.com/whaledone/index.cfm
3. Self-directed
    http://www.pfdf.org/leaderbooks/senge/fifth-discipline.html
4. Motivated
    http://bookstore.myleadercenter.com/n-0310208157.htm
5. Empowered
    http://www.empowermentresources.com
6. Self-actualized
    http://web.utk.edu/~gwynne/maslow.HTM

Responses to the posted assignment from fellow learners:

This is great. How do you find all this?

Learner 1 response: A hobby of reading leadership books and training material. Training is a passion of mine. It always has been. I think I do this better than raising my own kids. There's no manual with them. :)

Those were great - I liked the positive relationship one the best.

Great resources, Angie. The Dewitt Jones site was beautiful!

Really neat posts! I like the ability to build positive relationships the best. I think I may order that book.

I really enjoy Ken Blanchard. He seems practical and down to earth. His material is very applicable.

Learner 2 Post

This was fun. I found some good sites that I can definitely use. This is a great exercise for a trainer looking for some new stuff!! Not to mention getting to see everyone else's sites.

Here we will create a personal definition of excellence in terms of training. First think about what excellent training means to you personally. Then post a list of several characteristics that come to mind.

To me, excellent training is when I leave an event having learned what I came to and in the process enjoyed the session and was unaware of how and when I learned what I did. When I leave I'm thinking, I'd really like to come back to another one of so-and-so's classes!

Get My Attention

When I attend a training class, I know right off the bat whether I'm going to enjoy it or not. Being a trainer makes me a very critical participant. I try not to be but. . . When someone immediately gets my attention and does so in an interesting way I stop evaluating them and start listening!
http://www.educationworld.com/a_tech/tech166.shtml

Listening to a Great Speaker

I love listening to a great speaker. This also is something you know right away when listening. Last May during the Roosevelt graduation the guest speaker got up to speak. As soon as he said ten words I knew I was going to enjoy listening to him. I feel the same way in the classroom.
http://www.selfgrowth.com/articles/Allen21.html

Have Fun

There's nothing like getting so caught up in an activity that you're unaware of exactly how much you're learning. It's amazing to me how when students are having fun and are completely "in to" an activity they are able to retain so much

information. Even weeks later! So when it's time to apply the information to their jobs, it's still there.
http://trainme.org/train.htm

Prepared and Organized

Training is a lot of work. I've had people say to me, "I want your job, it looks so easy." I take that as a compliment since I know how much work it involves. If it looks easy then it must be running smoothly.
http://www.lin.ca/lin/resource/html/sp0056.pdf

Knowledgeable

This one is essential. The trainer doesn't need to be an expert. As a matter of fact I dread being trained by someone who knows everything about their subject and nothing about adult learning! This being said, the facilitator needs to have a solid and current background of their subject.

Finding one website is tough since the subject matter will dictate the sites. The most important thing is staying current in the subject matter of the industry. Below I list a few. . .

Manufacturing
http://www.industryweek.com/CurrentArticles/asp/articles.asp?ArticleID5410

E-Learning
http://www.thelearningsite.net/cyberlibrarian/elibraries/cybecurr.html

Law
http://www.llrx.com/features/keeping.htm

Analogies

I like a great analogy. If a concept is on the verge of making sense and someone throws in a great analogy, I'll get it. It also helps if I'm way off target by letting me know I'm going down the wrong thought process.
http://innovationworks.hypermart.net/i-analogy.htm
http://fp.bio.utk.edu/skeptic/handouts/rationalism-by-analogy.pdf
http://www.skillsplusinc.com/PDF%20Files/Icebreak.pdf

Strong Closing

There is nothing more awkward than a weak closing of a great training session. I tell my new trainers that if your participants are asking, "Can we go now, are we done?" then they probably need to work on their closings. My analogy for this is when you see a really good movie but the ending was dumb. First and last impressions can be strong allies or foes for life.
http://www.bobpikegroup.com/support/free/notrainer.html
http://www.goforstyle.com/calendar.html

Responses to the posted assignment from fellow learners:

Great job! I agree with you regarding listening to trainers who are subject matter experts, but have no adult learning or delivery skills.

Outstanding resources! I'm going to have a hard time getting this week's assignments done because I'm too busy exploring all the great websites that got posted for last week's assignment.

I love analogies—they really help me learn! Great sites!

ENDNOTES

1. E. D. Wagner, "In support of a functional definition of interaction," *The American Journal of Distance Education* 8 (1994): 6–26.

2. T. Duffy & D. Jonassen, *Constructives and the Technology of Instruction: A Conversation* (Hilldale, NJ: Lawrence Erlbaum Associates, 1996).

3. C. P. Fulford & S. Zhang, "Perceptions of interaction: The critical predictor in distance education," *The American Journal of Distance Education* 7 (1993): 8–21.

4. D. C. Hillman, D. J. Willis, & C. N. Gunawardena, "Learner interface interaction in distance education: An extension of contemporary models and strategies for practitioners," *The American Journal of Distance Education* 8 (1994): 30–42.

5. G. Moore, "Three types of interaction," *The American Journal of Distance Education* 3 (1989): 1–6.

6. Hillman, Willis, & Gunawardena (1994): 31–42.

7. L. L. Lohr, "Designing the instruction interface," *Computers in Human Behavior* 16 (2000): 161–182.

8. Moore (1989).

9. R. E. Clark, "Media will never influence learning," *Educational Technology Research and Development* 42 (1994b): 21–29.

10. S. Stoney & R. Oliver, "Developing interactive multimedia programs for higher education," *Association for the Advancement of Computing in Education* (June 1997): 23–31.

11. D. Vogel, "E-learning 1.0: Themes add creative spark to online classes," *ASTD Learning Circuits* (September 30, 2002): http://www.learningcircuits.org/2002/sep2002/ elearn.html

12. L. Millbower, "The auditory advantage," *ASTD Learning Circuits* (January 13, 2003): http://www.learningcircuits.org/2003/jan2003/millbower.htm

13. E. C. Thach & K. L. Murphy, "Competencies for distance education professionals," *Educational Technology Research and Development* 43 (1995): 57–79.

14. Moore (1989): 4.

15. Z. Berge, "Interaction in post-secondary web-based learning," *Educational Technology* 39 (1999): 5–11.

16. P. T. Northrup, "A framework for designing interactivity in web-based instruction," *Educational Technology* 41 (2001): 31–39.

17. Y. Kafai & M. Resnik, *Constructivism in Practice: Designing, Thinking, and Learning in a Digital World* (Mahwah, NJ: Lawrence Erlbaum Associates, 1996).

18. J. Novak & B. Gowin, *Learning How to Learn* (Cambridge: Cambridge University Press, 1984).

19. H. G. Schmidt, "Foundations of problem based learning," *Medical Education* 27 (1993): 422–432.

20. T. Duffy & D. Jonassen (Eds.), *Constructivism and the Technology of Instruction: Conversation* (Hillsdale, NJ: Lawrence Erlbaum Associates, 1992).

21. E. Foote, "Collaborative learning in community colleges," *ERIC Clearinghouse for Community Colleges*, Los Angeles, (1997): ED411023.

22. S. Papert, *The Children's Machine: Rethinking Schools in the Age of the Computer* (New York: Basic Books, 1993).

23. R. F. Mager, *Preparing Instructional Objectives* (Belmont, CA: David S. Lake, 1984).

24. Mager (1984).

25. M. Sheinberg, "E-learning 1.0 know thy learner: The importance of context in e-learning design," *ASTD Learning Circuits* (October 2001): http://www.learningcircuits.org/2001/oct2001/elearn.html

26. Sheinberg (2001).

27. B. Burke, "10 e-learning lessons: Please the customer or fail the course," *E Learning* 1 (2001): 40–41.

28. S. Cogen & D. Payiatakis, "E learning: Harnessing the hype," *Performance Improvement* 41 (2002): 7–15.

29. E. L. Deci & R. M. Ryan, *Intrinsic Motivation and Self-determination in Human Behavior* (New York: Plenum Press, 1985).

30. J. M. Keller, "Motivational design of instruction," in C. M. Reigeluth (Ed.), *Instructional Design Theories and Models: An Overview of Their Current Status* (Hillsdale, NJ: Lawrence Erlbaum Associates, 1983).

31. J. M. Keller, "Strategies for stimulating the motivation to learn," *Performance and Instruction* 26 (October 1987a): 1–7.

32. R. Gagne, *The Conditions of Learning* (New York: Holt, Rinehart & Winston, 1985).

33. B. Pike & C. Busse, *101 More Games for Trainers* (Minneapolis: Lakewood Books, 1995), 63.

34. B. Duch, D. Allen, & H. White, "Problem-based learning: Preparing learners to succeed in the 21st century," *Essays on Teaching Excellence* 9 (1999): http://www.unm.edu/~castl/Castl_Docs/Packet2/Problem-based%20Learning.html

35. H. Schmidt & H. Moust, "Factors affecting small group tutorial learning: A review of research," in D. G. Evensen & C. E. Hmelo (Eds.), *Problem Based Learning* (Mahwah, NJ: Lawrence Erlbaum Associates, 2000).

36. R. M. Purcell-Robertson & D. F. Purcell, "Interactive distance learning," in L. Lau (Ed.), *Distance Learning Technologies: Issues, Trends, and Opportunities* (Hershey, PA: Idea Group Publishing 2000), 16–21.

37. R. Clark & R. Mayer, *E-Learning and the Science of Instruction* (San Francisco: Jossey-Bass/Pfieffer, 2003), 219.

38. Pike & Busse, (1995), 62.

39. C. C. Bonwell & J. A. Eison, *Active Learning: Creating Excitement in the Classroom* (Washington, DC: George Washington University, 1991).

40. G. H. Turnwald, K. S. Bull, & D. C. Seeler: "From teaching to learning: Part II. Traditional teaching methodology," *Journal of Veterinary Medicine Education* 20 (1993): 148–156; N. J. Entwistle & P. Ramsden, *Understanding Student Learning* (London: Nicols Publishing Co, 1983).

41. Pike & Busse, (1995), 98.

42. B. Dodge, "Some thoughts about webquests," *The Distance Educator* 1 (1997): 12–15.

43. S. Thiagarajan, "Zero cost e-learning," *Learning Circuits* (May 2002): http://www.learningcircuits.org/2002/may2002/thiagi.html

INDEX